# ATTRACTING INVESTORS

# ATTRACTING INVESTORS

**A MARKETING APPROACH TO FINDING
FUNDS FOR YOUR BUSINESS**

Philip Kotler
Hermawan Kartajaya
S. David Young

WILEY

John Wiley & Sons, Inc.

Published by John Wiley & Sons, Inc., Hoboken, New Jersey.
Published simultaneously in Canada.

For general information on our other products and services please contact our Customer Care Department within the United States at (800) 762-2974, outside the United States at (317) 572-3993 or fax (317) 572-4002.

Wiley also publishes its books in a variety of electronic formats. Some content that appears in print may not be available in electronic books. For more information about Wiley products, visit our web site at www.Wiley.com.

*Library of Congress Cataloging-in-Publication Data:*
Kotler, Philip.
    Attracting investors : a marketing approach to finding funds for your
business / Philip Kotler, Hermawan Kartajaya, and S. David Young.
        p.   cm.
    ISBN 0-471-64656-3 (cloth)
    1. Venture capital.   2. Small business—Finance.   3. New business
enterprises—Finance.   I. Kartajaya, Hermawan, 1947–   II. Young, S. David.   III.
Title.
    HG4751.K68   2004
    658.15'224—dc22                                                          2004008610

Printed in the United States of America.

10  9  8  7  6  5  4  3  2  1

# CONTENTS

v

CONTENTS

# PREFACE

## THE PROBLEM:
## YOUR BUSINESS NEEDS MONEY

"It's money that makes the world go around." Every existing business firm and start-up firm needs money. Money must be borrowed to support payroll, material, equipment, and other costs before any revenue materializes.

If you picked up this book you may be an entrepreneur who is burning with a hot idea. You will importune family, friends, neighbors, venture capital firms, and banks for help. You will promise a several-fold return. You will argue that this is not charity, but a chance for the investor to make money while helping you build a great new business.

Or you may be an existing small business owner who runs into a cash flow problem. You will rush to your bank pleading for an extension of credit. You will need to make the best case to convince the bank that you will be able to pay back its funds with interest! You might have to seek out another bank, or friends, family, or neighbors for financial aid to carry your business through the crisis.

Or you may be part of a rapidly growing large firm that

needs substantial amounts of cash to build new factories and open new markets. If you are the company's financial vice president it is your job to envision the best mix of investor sources—commercial banks, investment banks, stock issues, debentures, and so on—to pursue. You have to demonstrate that the company's growth is real and will amply reward the investors.

Finally, you may belong to a large company that is in deep trouble. Your company badly needs money but is seen as a poor risk. Investors will be available but at a high cost of capital. How do troubled firms attract capital at a not too ruinous cost?

## THE SOLUTION: MARKETING

We believe that marketing concepts can help all these types of firms do a better job of attracting the funds they need. Our answer is not to knock on every possible investor's door in the hope of finally finding a benefactor. Marketing theory and practice involve a highly disciplined approach to identifying the best sources of capital and convincing them of a high reward-to-risk ratio in lending their funds. This book will explain the different sources of funds and how investors and lenders decide whom to back from among competing borrowers. Once you understand how different types of investors and lenders think, you can identify your business's best prospects and make your best case for financial assistance. Every businessperson is ultimately competing for capital and must market with hard facts and convincing arguments.

PREFACE

The first part of this book is an introduction and overview of the capital markets. The second part describes how capital markets operate. The third part describes how marketing concepts and tools can aid in the process of attracting the capital that you need for your business.

Good sailing in the money waters!

Philip Kotler
Hermawan Kartajaya
S. David Young

# PART ONE

# INTRODUCTION

# 1

# Marketing to Investors and Lenders: What the Capital Markets Want

WHAT INVESTORS WANT

TRENDS IN RAISING CAPITAL

    Globalization

    Advances in Technology

    Financial Innovation

    Changes in Attitudes toward Savings and Investment

    Growing Dominance of Institutional Investors

Until recently, entrepreneurs or corporate managers who needed to raise capital had limited options. Money from investors and banks did not flow freely to the businesses that could most profitably invest it because there were always regulatory, institutional, cultural, or technological barriers that restricted capital flows. Now all of this has changed. It is easier to get funding from international sources because the foreign exchange controls that limited flows from one currency to another largely disappeared a generation ago. It is easier to sell stock in your company because stock exchanges have made it easy for investors to get into and out of financial markets. Plus, attitudes to investing have undergone profound changes as a whole new generation of investors, in the United States and elsewhere, have discovered the attractions of stock ownership; and extraordinary advances in information technology have helped to break down some of the technical barriers to the free flow of capital.

What all of this means is that massive sums of capital can move toward your company, or away from it, in the blink of an eye. As economists predicted as far back as the nineteenth century, when capital *can* flow, it *will* flow. What we are witnessing now is the realization of that vision.

What are the consequences of these developments to corporate managers or to entrepreneurs who seek to raise capital? Very simply, it means that they must convince investors and lenders, who now have a virtually limitless array of investment opportunities available in markets all over the world, to invest money in their firms. To be most effective, this persuasion must draw on the power and tools of marketing.

While this point seems obvious at first, let's consider the practical effects of it. Thanks to recent capital market developments, investors can put their money practically anywhere. Just as companies must convince potential customers that they offer a superior value proposition compared to competing firms, or else customers will take their business elsewhere, companies needing capital must do likewise for investors; they must compete for capital. Part of this requires marketing their cases effectively to the right capital providers. But unlike commercial markets, in capital markets the firm needing money doesn't just do battle with its industry competitors.

Modern finance theory tells us that investors seek the highest risk-adjusted returns from their invested capital. Notice that they don't seek the highest gross returns. If that were the case, no one would invest in conservative, mainstream companies. Instead, they seek the highest returns on a risk-adjusted basis. Finance professionals normally define this risk in terms of stock price volatility, although the basic principle applies also to companies that aren't publicly traded. Simply put, investors want the highest returns possible for a given level of risk or price volatility, or the least risk or volatility for a given level of expected returns. This means that when companies compete for the loyalty of investors, they don't compete only in their industry; they compete against all other companies of comparable risk.

In fact, the challenge is even more daunting. Investors can temper the volatility of a high-risk company by adding low-risk investments, such as government bonds, to their portfolios. For example, an investment in a risky, high-tech venture, when combined with U.S. Treasury bills, may offer the same net risk profile as Procter & Gamble. If that investment combination is thought by investors to offer the prospect of higher returns than P&G's shares, investors will naturally prefer that alternative. In other words, Procter & Gamble doesn't compete for capital just against Johnson & Johnson and other important sector players; it also competes against firms in a broad range of industries, and not just firms with a similar risk profile. And with the increasing globalization of the world's capital markets, the competition for capital is played out on a worldwide stage.

Complicating matters even further is another key difference between capital markets and commercial markets. Capital markets (more specifically, stock markets) have players with no real interest in the product per se (in this case, companies). These speculators trade with no interest in the subject companies except to capture profits from short-term price movements. In many markets, these speculators can account for most of the trading in stocks (although rarely do they account for most of the ownership). This creates an important, and confusing, source of noise that garbles the message the capital markets are sending to companies on how their performance and future potential are perceived.

For a publicly traded firm, the stock market is the single most important source of information available about what investors think of it. In the world's largest exchanges, the market sends messages continually, combining investors' expectations of the future with reaction to news and rumors. In short, the market is both predictive and reactive. While it reacts to the events of the moment, it also anticipates the future—sometimes accurately, sometimes not. Also, stock exchanges are notoriously fickle, with price movements often the result of fads, moods, euphoria, or panic. But as the legendary investor Warren Buffett says, "Value will out." This means that, sooner or later, the market sorts through the information and noise, and rewards those companies with the greatest potential for generating shareholder wealth.

## WHAT INVESTORS WANT

The guiding principles of investment decision making are (1) more benefits, in the form of profits or cash flow, are preferred to less; (2) near-term benefits are preferred to more distant benefits; and (3) safe investments are preferred to risky ones. Although it's easy to fall into the trap that somehow the basic principles of investment are different in start-up ventures than in large, mature companies, these principles apply to all investments, in all markets, and for all investors. As we show in the next chapter, however, the ways in which the essential features of this framework are applied will vary according to the stage of a firm's development as well as other factors.

When someone invests capital in a business, any business, that investment invariably takes the form of cash, or at least something that is convertible into cash. To illustrate, suppose a company's share price is $50, and that a particular investor owns 1,000 shares. By phoning his (or her) stockbroker, the investor could convert those shares into $50,000 of cash. Why doesn't he? The logical answer is that he believes, rightly or wrongly, that by holding on to the shares he will receive cash from the investment in the future that has a present value equivalent greater than $50,000. If he didn't believe this, the only

7

logical course of action would be to bail out of the company and put the cash somewhere else.

This simple example points out several important lessons about capital markets and how customers in capital markets (i.e., investors) go about the business of deciding where to invest their resources. First, it shows that the value of any investment is based on the future and not the past. If investors have cash tied up in the company today, which must be true because their investments can be converted into cash in the present simply by issuing sell orders to their brokers, they do so because of expectations that they will receive more cash in the future by hanging on to their shares. The past still matters because it helps investors to form expectations of the future, but ultimately it is only expectations of the future and not realizations of the past that determine the value of any company.

The second key lesson is that value is based on capital market expectations of performance. The practical consequence of this lesson is that value is driven by the beliefs of investors and potential investors. A company can be blessed with the world's best managers and value-creating strategies, but unless the capital markets believe it there is no value creation. When it comes to valuation, if the capital markets don't believe it, it's not true. This fundamental reality points out the central role of communications in affecting market perceptions of value and risk.

Third, because investors tie up cash in the present, it is the prospect of getting even more cash in the future that gives companies any value at all in the capital markets. This is why finance professionals place so much emphasis on cash flows. Companies have value precisely because they can deliver cash flows to investors in the future. Those companies that are not perceived as having that ability are unable to raise capital.

8

More specifically, the cash flow investors care about is called "free cash flow." It's normally defined as a company's operating cash flows (i.e., the cash generated from its day-to-day business activities), net of whatever investment is required to sustain and grow these cash flows. The remainder, or free cash flow, represents the amount of cash that the company will then be able to give to its shareholders, bankers, and bond-holders. In other words, it is the cash flow left over, after investment, for distribution to capital providers. Because capital providers invest in companies precisely because of the prospect of future cash rewards, and free cash flow represents the cash the company will be able to give back, the value of any business must be a function of its perceived ability to generate free cash flows in the future. This does not mean that free cash flows have to be positive this year, or even next, for a company to have value now. It only means that investors must believe in the company's ability to generate positive free cash flows in the future. If investors do not believe this is possible, to them the company has no value now.

The fourth, and final, lesson this example teaches us is that because any cash flows that a company might provide its investors will appear in the future, all such cash flows must be discounted. The discounting process, which reflects both the time value of money and the risk that the expected cash flows might not materialize, allows investors to convert a stream of expected benefits (to be received at different points in the future) into a common point of reference called the present value equivalent. In short, future free cash flows are discounted by a cost of capital, or interest rate, that reflects the rate of return that investors would expect if they invested in another company of similar risk.

As we show in the following chapter, while the basic aim of investing is the same for any investor, namely the highest risk-adjusted returns on capital, the cast of characters changes dramatically as companies make the transition from private to public ownership. Logically, therefore, publicly traded companies market themselves differently than start-ups or growth companies that have not yet gone public. For example, the market for venture capital or angel investing is of little or no interest to Cola-Cola or Intel. Instead, their sales efforts in the capital markets are targeted mainly at large institutional investors in the mutual fund, pension fund, and insurance industries.

While the dominant motive for investing is the desire to earn competitive returns, there can be other motives, too. For example, some investors in start-up or early-stage investments are attracted by the opportunity to play a role in the entrepreneurial process. They may have been successful entrepreneurs themselves, and welcome the chance to play that role again. The free time and financial security provided by earlier successes gives them the means to do this. Altruism can play a part, too, especially for investors who want to "give something back" to their local communities or hometowns. They may hope to stimulate investment or entrepreneurial activity in the region by offering capital and expertise to budding entrepreneurs. But while these motives can sometimes play a role in the allocation of capital, their importance is overwhelmed by the desire of capital providers to earn the highest risk-adjusted returns possible on their capital.

Although the world's capital markets are bigger than ever, the competition for capital has never been greater than it is now. With so many businesses competing for this capital, the process of raising capital has become as much of a marketing function as a finance function. Logically, therefore, the key elements of marketing come into play. For example, "know your market." This means understanding who your best prospective investors (buyers) are, what they want to know, and what sort of investment opportunities they look for. Trying to sell a security to the wrong prospective buyer is expensive and wasteful, particularly when the range of tastes for securities covers virtually every kind of company and every kind of industry.

Another tenet of marketing is to "know your product." This means knowing every aspect of what your business has to offer investors. What can you offer them, in terms of risk-adjusted returns, that other investment opportunities cannot? In order to compete successfully for capital, any company must be prepared to demonstrate—clearly, forcefully, and honestly—those factors about itself that indicate why it would be such a good investment.

Another tenet of marketing is to "know how to communicate effectively." One of the authors attended an investor forum where would-be entrepreneurs had 10 minutes each to explain their business concepts and risk-return prospects. Half of the presentations were so poorly done that they didn't stand a chance, however good their business concept might have been.

Today, managers talk about creating a value proposition for their customers. They must do likewise for their capital providers. In short, they must convince investors that their business offers a superior risk-return profile (i.e., a superior value proposition) to alternative investment opportunities (i.e., competitors).

# TRENDS IN RAISING CAPITAL

Capital markets have undergone profound changes over the past generation, and we are confident that they will continue to do so in the future. Anyone hoping to raise substantial amounts of capital these days should have at least some understanding of these changes and the trends behind them. The most important trends include globalization, technological advances, financial innovations, changes in savings and investment, and dominance of institutional investors.

## Globalization

Capital markets are now global. This trend has been spurred by a number of events and circumstances, beginning with the gradual disappearance of exchange controls in the 1970s. Throughout the 1980s and 1990s, deregulation was the major contributing factor. Today, capital tends to flow to countries where the risk-return trade-offs are attractive and restrictions on inflows and outflows are small. As countries have opened up their markets to foreign issuers seeking capital and to foreign investors seeking outlets for their investment dollars (or euros or yen), companies and investors have responded with massive capital flows. In turn, countries now find it hard to maintain highly restricted capital markets because the key players can avoid these restrictions simply by doing business elsewhere.

In one important area, however, regulation has actually increased. Where previously regulation was designed primarily to stifle markets, more recently policy makers have striven to make securities trading a fairer game. As a result, insider trading rules have been strengthened, especially in Europe where, until recently, insider trading prosecutions were extremely rare. Also, recent accounting scandals notwithstanding, corporate disclosure requirements have increased, making it easier for investors to track and compare the performances of publicly traded companies.

Large multinational corporations routinely raise debt and equity capital outside their home countries, but these days even smaller companies are moving beyond their home country borders to lure investors. This trend is largely a positive one because it gives companies access to much broader pools of capital, and it also allows companies to take advantage of differences in taxes and regulations across countries, thereby lowering their cost of capital. However, globalization also means that companies compete for capital not just against industry or national rivals, but also against investment opportunities outside their home markets. The increased fluidity of capital can be both a benefit and a curse.

## Advances in Technology

The most important reality of today's capital markets is that huge amounts of capital can flow from one company to another, from one instrument to another, and from one country to another, practically in the blink of an eye. These capital flows would not be possible without the processing power offered by today's computer technologies. These technologies make it possible to simultaneously issue billions of dollars of securities in several countries around the world, to trade trillions of dollars of securities on stock exchanges and other trading platforms, and to efficiently price new instruments as they reach the market. We are now converging to a truly continuous, 24-hour global trading regime, at least for the equity of the world's largest, best-known companies. Eventually, such trading opportunities will extend to a much broader range of securities.

## Financial Innovation

Globalization, deregulation, and information technology have spurred the creation of innovative financial instruments. Investment bankers have designed new instruments that allow companies to (1) tailor securities that appeal to a well-defined set of investors, (2) reduce the effects of fluctuating interest and exchange rates, and (3) convert illiquid assets into highly liquid financial instruments. The result is an astonishing array of financial instruments available in global capital markets.

An important example of such innovation is the growth of securitization, a trend that began to accelerate in the 1980s. This is the process of combining assets or financial instruments that are not securities, registering the combined, or bundled, units as securities, and selling them directly to the public. Securitization practically revolutionized the mortgage market in the United States by creating publicly traded mortgage instruments. The practice was later extended to cover a broad range of assets, leading to a whole new market in asset-backed securities. For example, companies can now sell their trade receivables, and raise much needed capital, at lower cost than before.

An interesting consequence of financial innovation is that it has helped to blur the lines that distinguish one type of financial institution from the others. For example, as we explore in Chapter 5, commercial banks aren't the only institutions providing commercial loans. Insurance companies, pension funds, and other investor types are in the business, too. Similarly, securitization and similar innovations have allowed other institutions to compete on turf that previously belonged exclusively to investment banks.

## Changes in Attitudes toward Savings and Investment

While all of these developments took shape, a new generation of investors emerged, flush with cash and possessed as well of more favorable attitudes toward capital market investing than earlier generations. Aided by a seemingly endless bull market (interrupted by the odd crash, such as in 1987 or in 2000 with the collapse of technology stocks) and solid evidence that with a long enough investment horizon a person is almost certainly better off investing in equities than in government bonds or bank accounts, millions of people whose parents never even thought about buying stocks have taken the plunge and become shareholders. This trend was accelerated in Europe by privatization campaigns that sought to ensure the permanence of private ownership by encouraging dispersion of the shares of newly privatized companies among a large cross section of citizens.

## Growing Dominance of Institutional Investors

Interest in stocks, and in investing generally, has grown in ways unimaginable to finance professionals as recently as the 1970s. The result is a veritable worldwide explosion in mutual funds, unit trusts, and other forms of institutional investment. Not only do many more people have a financial stake in companies, typically through mutual funds or pension funds, but of particular importance to corporate managers is that these funds are run by professional managers who care only about

15

performance and delivering the highest returns possible to the people who hired them. There is little doubt that the explosion in pension fund investing over the past generation, and the growth of professional money management that came with it, is the single greatest factor behind the emphasis on shareholder value creation in U.S. companies.

This trend is beginning to intensify in Europe, too, thanks in part to its own mutual fund industry but also because of the growth of pension funds. With aging populations and an unsustainable safety net, a growing number of Europeans now recognize that underfunded social security programs will be unable to serve the retirement needs of today's workforce. To provide for the needs of an aging population, and to stimulate savings and corporate investment, many countries have implemented or are planning to implement pension and savings plans that will channel unprecedented amounts of equity capital to European companies.

# 2

# Raising Capital: An Overview of Your Alternatives

At its most basic level, capital exists in two forms: debt and equity. Debt finance comes primarily from bank loans and bonds, although supplier finance and loans from development banks or other institutions may also be available. Equity comes mainly in the form of common stock, but preferred equity and warrants are sometimes used. Hybrid instruments, which combine aspects of debt and equity, have become especially popular in recent years.

The main difference between debt and equity lies in the nature of their claims on the firm's cash flows. While debt holders such as bankers and bondholders have fixed claims in the form of interest and principal payments, equity investors have residual claims. They get paid only after all other claimants have been satisfied. Also, debt holders have a priority of claim in the event of liquidation, while equity holders have the lowest priority of all claimants. Another important difference is that the interest paid to debt holders is tax deductible for the company while dividend payments to shareholders are not. In addition, debt nearly always has a fixed maturity that means that at some point the principal has to be paid. Equity, in contrast, has an infinite life. And finally, equity holders have rights of management control, or at least the right to elect directors who will choose the firm's managers. Except in cases of financial distress, debt holders normally exert no control over management.

Financing choices can be thought of as lying on a continuum, with the fixed claims, high priority, tax deductibility, fixed maturity, and lack of management control associated with debt at one end, and the residual claims, low priority, non–tax deductibility, infinite life, and management control associated with equity at the other. Hybrids lie somewhere between the two extremes, which means that they simultaneously share the characteristics of both debt and equity.

Convertible bonds, which are bonds that can be converted into a predetermined number of shares of common stock at the discretion of the investor, are the most popular form of hybrid. Finance professionals normally view such instruments as multiple securities, with a debt component (in this case, the "straight" bond, or the bond without the conversion feature) and an equity component (the option to buy common stock). Convertible debt is an especially attractive alternative to straight debt for high-growth companies that do not yet have high operating cash flows. The high growth and risk of the business drive up the value of the call feature, which reduces the amount of interest that the company must pay on the bond. Of course, no financing vehicle works unless it is also attractive to investors. Convertible bonds provide investors with predictable and contractually guaranteed interest payments, while also giving them the possibility of participating in the upside in case the firm really takes off.

## FACTORS INFLUENCING THE SOURCES OF CAPITAL

With innovations in the world's capital markets, the range of prospective financing sources is quite extensive these days and still growing. The following is just a partial list of the financing sources available:

| | |
|---|---|
| Angel financing. | Leasing. |
| Asset-based lending. | Personal savings. |
| Bootstrapping. | Public debt issue. |
| Customer financing. | Research and development |
| Factoring. | (R&D) limited partnerships. |
| Franchising. | Secondary rights offerings. |
| Friends and family. | Unsecured bank lending. |
| Initial public | Vendor financing. |
| offering (IPO). | Venture capital. |

Why are there so many choices? As the convertible bond example suggests, they serve the interests of both investors and the corporate users of capital. For investors, alternatives make capital markets more "complete," which is a term used by financial economists to mean that risk-return opportunities are broadened. Simply put, investment vehicles catch on because they make it possible for investors to earn higher returns on their portfolios without increasing risk, or to reduce risk without sacrificing returns. As for businesses, a broad array of financing alternatives allows for choices that are well suited to their particular characteristics and needs. In other words, different kinds of businesses have different financing needs. These needs may be small or large, and short- or long-term. One business may be capable of offering a high degree of safety, whereas another may require the investor to bear considerable risk. Businesses also differ in their tax exposures, management capabilities, needs for flexibility, and many other dimensions. Another reason for so many financing alternatives is that capital providers have different objectives, capabilities, and constraints. Some, like banks, prefer low-involvement, low-risk investment, usually of a short duration. Others, like business angels, seek high-risk, high-involvement investments of a medium- to long-term duration. In some cases, financing is closely linked to aspects of the business such as distribution, marketing, and sourcing. This is especially true for customer- and vendor-provided financing. Also, different financing sources protect the value of their investments in different ways. Some sources, like venture capitalists (VCs), engage in active monitoring to protect their investments. Others, like factoring companies and most lenders, rely heavily on collateral.

But the single greatest influence on the financing vehicles sought by a company is its stage of development. The start-up stage, for example, represents the highest level of business risk because of numerous uncertainties about whether the product to be offered will work as expected; if it does work, whether prospective customers will buy it; if it is accepted, whether the volumes sold and the revenues earned will more than compensate for the development and launch costs; and, even if all this works, whether the company will gain enough market share to justify its continued involvement in the industry. Because of this high level of *business* risk, the *financial* risk (namely, the extent to which the company relies on debt to finance its assets) must be kept low. Thus some form of equity funding is most appropriate, but the financing options are limited. The high risk of the venture limits its attractiveness to a relatively small group of investors. In fact, the largest pools of capital available (e.g., mutual funds, insurance company portfolios, and pension funds) are prevented either by regulation or by their own bylaws from investing in such ventures.

The ideal equity investor for start-ups must understand the risks involved, including the very real possibility of total loss. Investors must also expect to receive their returns in the form of a capital gain when they exit from the investment; dividends are rarely a realistic option for such companies. Nearly all serious venture capitalists (i.e., those with the most capital to invest) are professional investors who not only accept and understand the high risk involved in any specific investment, but can also mitigate that risk by developing a portfolio of similarly high-risk projects. The idea is that the failure of some investments is more than offset by the great success of others.

Raising capital is very different, of course, in large, established companies, especially those with publicly traded equity. Besides the obvious difference in scale, the creditworthiness of large companies gives them financing options not normally available to smaller businesses, such as unsecured (i.e., noncollateralized) debt.

Also, investors in public companies realize returns in the form of dividends and from capital gains that arise when shares of stock are sold to other investors. The investors' decisions to sell are essentially independent of a company's investment activities. In their decisions to invest in the shares of a public corporation, investors normally give little consideration to when they will sell or to the costs associated with selling.

Investing in new ventures is different. New venture investments normally are not liquid and often do not generate significantly positive free cash flow for several years. Most investors in new ventures, and many entrepreneurs, have finite investment horizons. To realize the returns on their investments, a "liquidity event" must occur. Such liquidity events are the main ways investors in new ventures harvest, or realize, the returns on their investments. Because of the importance of liquidity events, they generally are explicitly forecast. Such forecasts are not needed for more mature businesses that are already publicly traded.

The dominant source of finance for publicly traded firms, and often for private businesses, too, is internal financing in the form of reinvested profits. A review of the Compustat database, which provides detailed financial information on thousands of companies, shows that internal financing over the past 30 years has accounted for between 60 and 80 percent of total financing for medium-sized and large firms. Firms of all sizes, public as well as private, typically prefer internal financing because internally generated cash flows can be used to finance growth without the issuance costs or loss of managerial flexibility that can come with external financing.

When firms are unable to finance all desired investments from their internal sources, they resort to external funds. Debt finance tends to be preferred to equity, accounting for between 15 percent and 25 percent of total financing. New issues of equity make up the rest, only rarely exceeding 10 percent of the total.

While it's true that the equity markets supply only a portion of the total capital needed by corporations, equity's contribution to total capital formation is far greater than just its dollar value. First, the contribution by equity represents a significant segment of total capital in terms of the way it is used. It acts more often as a base for all other financing. Debt finance is not a realistic possibility unless there is a cushion of equity capital in the company. One reason why we care about the value of equity is that it influences debt-equity ratios. Finance theory says that the true indebtedness of a company can be understood only by reference to the market values of the capital claims held against it. When the value of

23

equity declines, the ability of the company to borrow may be impaired. Or at least the company may have to pay more for debt finance it does obtain.

Also, at the time equity is raised, especially in an initial public offering, it often moves the company from one level of operations to another. While normal operational growth can frequently be financed from retained earnings, new equity issues are used for the spurt, for the significant expansion of either operations or markets, or for the acquisition program that sharply increases the size of the company.[1]

To summarize, the methods of financing depend on a firm's size, growth prospects, cash flows, and risk. Put another way, the funds-raising process depends on a firm's place in its life cycle. As firms grow and mature, and as their risk profiles change, so too do the ways in which they raise capital. For example, cash flows from operations tend to increase for maturing businesses, while risk (which at first is very high) tends to converge to an economy-wide average. The financing choices made by firms reflect these changes.

## HOW RAISING CAPITAL VARIES WITH A FIRM'S LIFE CYCLE

We now examine the process of raising capital at each stage of a company's life. To start, consider the stages of a firm's life cycle:

1. Start-up.
2. Expansion.
3. Post-IPO growth.

**4.** Low growth and maturity.

**5.** Decline.

## Start-Up

Start-up represents the initial stage after a business has been formed, and is normally reserved for businesses that are less than one year old. This stage normally begins with an R&D or "seed" phase, in which the entrepreneur focuses on product research and development activities and has not yet begun to invest in the assets required to initiate production and sale of the product or service. The venture generates no revenues during this period. The entrepreneur really just has a concept for a potentially profitable business that still has to be developed and proven.

In the next phase of the start-up stage, the firm begins to acquire the facilities, equipment, and employees that are required to produce the product and begin selling. Usually, such businesses are private, funded by contributions from the entrepreneur and perhaps friends and family of the entrepreneur. There may also be some reliance on bank debt, although banks are likely to lend only for investments in assets that can be used as collateral. Unsecured debt, or loans that are not backed by specific assets, is generally very difficult, if not impossible, to obtain at this stage because of the considerable risk that the business will not survive. At least in the case of asset-backed finance there is something for the bank to sell if the business fails.

Much of the financing at this stage is what is popularly known as "bootstrapping." The term is generally used to describe creative and unorthodox ways of raising finance, along with ways of running the business so as to minimize the need for capital. Examples of the former include the use of personal credit cards, second mortgages and other home equity loans, personal savings, and customer advances. Bootstrapping techniques to minimize the need for capital include buying used equipment and machinery instead of new, leasing assets instead of buying them, delaying or forgoing compensation, borrowing assets from other businesses, sharing premises with other businesses, working out of one's home or garage, and employing relatives and close friends at below-market salaries.

While bootstrapping is a popular and relatively low-cost approach for entrepreneurs to get their businesses off the ground, the obvious drawback is that these techniques quickly get stretched to their limits. Rapid expansion nearly always requires additional financing, except in those rare cases where a business becomes profitable so quickly that it can finance its growth from internal sources. But in most cases, if the reliance on bootstrapping continues, the firm can find itself competing poorly against well-endowed competitors, limiting its ability to gain sales and market share and to establish a strong overall competitive position within its target market.

Getting to the next stage of development requires external capital, usually in the form of private equity. The most common sources of private equity are business angels and venture capitalists. Although the line separating the two forms of investors is sometimes blurred, there are important differences. Angels tend to invest earlier in the life cycle of the business than VCs. Therefore, they are more likely than VCs to invest in the start-up phase. Also, they tend to invest as individuals or sometimes in syndicates of individuals, while VCs normally ply their trade in specialist venture capital firms that raise funds from other parties. In other words, while angels invest their own money, VCs typically invest someone else's. Another important difference is that the dollar amounts of venture capital investments tend to be far more substantial than those of angel investors. Angels rarely invest more than $1 million, even when working in syndicates; investments between $25,000 and $250,000 are the norm. By contrast, venture capital investments often run into the millions of dollars.

The funding restrictions of angels combined with the preferences of venture capitalists sometimes gives rise to what is known as the "equity gap." The problem tends to arise when ventures require between $250,000 and $500,000 in contributed capital, which is a common requirement for businesses that are just emerging from their bootstrapping stage of finance. The problem arises because while the amount is too high for most angels and beyond the reach of bootstrapping techniques, it is often too low for venture capitalists. Because the costs of appraising and monitoring investments can be considerable, investments below a certain size are uneconomic for VCs. But the high-risk nature of the business makes it a poor candidate for unsecured bank lending. The result is that the needed financing is not available in any form. The rapid growth of the venture capital industry in the late 1990s has probably reduced the severity of the problem at the top end of scale, while the rapid growth of angel investing has provided some relief at the bottom end, but the equity gap still exists.

By the time VCs have invested in a particular target, the company has achieved a greater level of sales and growth, and therefore a greater demand for capital, than it had when the angels first invested in it. Because more is at stake, the due diligence performed by a venture capitalist is generally far more extensive than that of an angel. Contracts, too, tend to be more comprehensive and detailed. Another important difference is that VCs put more emphasis than angels on exiting the firm, although all investors care about how they will capture any value creation realized by the business.

Venture capitalists tend to get most of the press coverage, but most entrepreneurial firms are funded by business angels, not VCs. One source estimates that angels fund 30 to 40 times more ventures each year than venture capitalists.[2] Angels have become such a popular source of funding for new ventures, in part, because the economic boom of the 1990s produced a record number of rich investors. In addition, there are important attractions to angel investing. For example, angel investments can be a good hedge against fluctuations in the stock market; the amounts required for individual investments are limited (when compared to venture capital); and investors can leverage their previous experience by funding and helping firms in areas they know quite a bit about, and thereby actually make a difference directly.[3] Many angels have started their own successful firms in the past and are now looking to invest some of their money and experience in small entrepreneurial ventures.

Angels participate based on their relevant experience, time availability, and preferences.[4] While some angels are silent partners, others take an active interest in the management of the company. For example, some angels act as members of the management team, on a full- or part-time basis. This enables a business to exploit the angel's functional expertise or personal contacts. In other cases, the angel is a coach, providing active advice and assistance, as needed, to the entrepreneur. Unlike the management team member, coaches stay on the sidelines, leaving day-to-day operating decisions to the full-time managers. This role tends to work only with angels who have considerable investing experience. A less common role for angels is to become the controlling manager.

Some angels merely dabble in the market for start-ups, while serious investors tend to take a more sophisticated port-folio approach. Angel investing is somewhat like drilling for oil. Even the best prospectors strike oil only 30 percent of the time. Therefore, a successful exploration strategy requires a di-versified approach. Diversification is just as important in the world of angel investing, where success rates of only 10 or 15 percent are common. Successful angel investors tend to invest in several businesses as a way of spreading the risk and increas-ing the likelihood that they will have a least one big winner.

Also, most angels tend to specialize by industry, limiting their investments to businesses and technologies they under-stand. In addition, angels usually limit the geographic range of their investments, because they tend to know more about mar-kets and business conditions in their home regions or countries.

## Expansion

Once a firm succeeds in attracting customers and establishing a presence in the market, it begins looking for the resources it will need to grow. In this stage, the firm is producing and de-livering products or services, but likely has been doing so for less than five years. It probably is not yet profitable, but even if there are profits, they are almost certainly insufficient to fi-nance rapid growth. Also, short operating histories and small firm size limit access to public securities markets. Instead, such firms rely initially on private equity, usually in the form of ven-ture capital, although some angels are active at this stage. The most successful of these businesses will later become publicly traded by issuing equity on stock exchanges or "over-the-counter" markets such as Nasdaq.

Most of the financing in this phase, up to initial public offerings, is accounted for by venture capitalists. To illustrate how the process of venture capital investment works, and to raise important issues that any capital-seeking entrepreneur is likely to face before the IPO stage, we draw on the example of Atila Ventures, a midsize venture capital firm based in Munich and Lausanne. As of early 2002, its staff of 12 professionals managed a fund of approximately $100 million for the firm's own account, and a similar amount on behalf of a large German manufacturer. Most of Atila's investments are in microelectronics, information technology, or data communications, reflecting the specialized technical expertise of its staff. Given the operational expertise of Atila's people, it tends to focus on what it calls "second-round" financing, that is, deals in which the target business has already received a previous round of venture capital. It does do first-round deals, however, and also invests in third-round, or pre-IPO, opportunities.

In assessing potential deals, Atila scores a venture on each of several criteria, including:

- Market opportunity.
- Competitive situation.
- Technology.
- Barriers to entry (such as patents).
- Quality of management.
- Brands and trademarks.
- Distribution networks.

- Administration and control.
- Stability of operations.
- Sales and profit consistency.
- Possibility of diversification vis-à-vis Atila's other investments.

According to Atila's admittedly subjective weighting scheme, the most important of these criteria is the quality of management, followed by barriers to entry.

The emphasis placed on the management team reflects the commonsense idea that quality managers not only suggest potential upside but also lower risk, a prime concern for investments where the inherent risks are already high. While the emphasis on management quality is common among venture capitalists, for most angels the entrepreneur is the greatest attraction to an investment.[5] Many plan to work with the entrepreneur for a number of years and so want to make sure that the individual is compatible and qualified. Angels invest in people, more so than in sectors or industries. Sometimes, though, angels will overlook some deficiencies in the skills of the venture's management, relying on their own skills to make up for any shortcomings. Because they tend to invest later in the life cycle of a business, venture capitalists are normally less forgiving on this point, often refusing to invest if a solid team of professional managers is not already in place.

The weighting, or influence, of each criterion by Atila's staff is based in part on whether the deal is first, second, or third round. For example, sales and profit consistency is an important factor for third-round deals, less important for second-round financing, and not considered at all in the first round.

31

In all cases, the result is a score somewhere between –60 and +60. Any opportunity with a score of 50 or greater is called a no-brainer or obvious "yes," while deals with scores between 25 and 49 are given serious consideration. Ventures with scores under 25 are rejected without further discussion.

Once the decision has been made to pursue the target, Atila then embarks on a four-step process to value the business and determine how much capital it is willing to invest. First, Atila's staff rewrites the target's business plan. Based on its own analysis of product markets, competition, and pricing, it develops what it considers realistic sales growth figures. Atila then estimates the costs and investments required to generate projected sales, which then yields profitability and cash flow forecasts. The rewriting of the business plan is used both as a basis for valuing the target and as ammunition for Atila in negotiating terms with the target management.

The second step in the process is to estimate a realistic long-term cash flow growth potential for the target. This is done by asking, "What will this business look like, and how profitable should it be, when it hits 'steady state'?" Normally, steady state is defined in terms of the venture's performance three to four years in the future, after which Atila would expect to have exited from the investment. Although Atila will no longer have a stake in the company, the steady state assumptions will be the critical factors driving its estimates of what it should be able to get for the business when it is time to leave.

This leads to step three, in which Atila defines an exit value—that is, what it would expect the business to be worth in three or four years. The exit value is based on discounted cash flows. The process is complete when, in step four, the company works backward from the exit value to derive an en-

32

try value, which is the maximum price the firm would be willing to pay for its piece of the target. This price is based on the time to exit (i.e., how many years Atila would expect to wait before cashing out) and the required rate of return. The required return is derived from the scoring model described earlier, with targets having scores of 50 or better assigned a 30 percent annual return. Lower scores signal higher risk, and therefore demand higher returns. For example, the riskiest projects Atila is willing to consider—those with scores of 25 to 30—are set targets of 100 percent. Projects of intermediate risk are assigned required returns of either 60 or 80 percent.

In short, all investments made by the firm are expected, *ex ante*, to earn between 30 and 100 percent annually. Based on the required return and the time to exit, the firm then calculates what it calls "uplift." The uplift represents the amount by which the value of Atila's initial investment must multiply for the firm to earn its required return. For example, the uplift is 4.1 if the time to exit is three years and the target return is 60 percent. This means that if the exit value is expected to be $4.1 million, the most that Atila would be willing to pay for its interest in the target is $1 million, or $4.1 million divided by the uplift factor of 4.1. If Atila were to pay this amount and cash out in three years at $4.1 million, it would have earned exactly 60 percent per year on its initial investment.

Although the return goals seem high, so, too, are the failure rates. The expectation is that the small number of big winners will more than offset the large number of losers. It should be noted, however, that failure rates for venture capitalists are lower than those for angels. One reason is that VCs tend to invest later in the life cycle of the business than angels, and thus some of the uncertainty of the target has been resolved, or at least reduced. Also, VCs are concentrated in highly professional firms. Angels do often cooperate with one another in the form of syndicates, and also may have industry expertise like VCs, but many angels take a more ad hoc or random approach to their deal making.

One increasingly popular approach is to rely on business brokers to sell the business. Essentially a variant of the management buy-in, specialists get listings from VCs and angels, receiving a commission each time they sell a company. The brokers value the business, market it to potential buyers, and even assist in the negotiations to bring buyer and seller together. This approach offers advantages to both the investors wanting to cash out and those wanting to buy in. For the seller, brokers can vet potential buyers, granting access to only serious investors with the necessary financial resources and a genuine interest in the target. For the buyer, they offer access to companies that the buyer would otherwise not know about. Also, some brokers provide valuable due diligence services.

Like most VC firms, Atila has strong regional preferences. Venture capital is a business that relies heavily on personal relationships and well-honed instincts. When VCs venture far from their usual stomping ground, they often lack the intuitive skills that are the foundation for successful investing. The practices that work in some places might not work in others. American VCs discovered this truth when they began turning to Europe in the aftermath of the Internet meltdown. Europe was seen as virgin territory with unlimited, but untapped, potential, reminding some VC pros of Silicon Valley in the 1980s. But to their disappointment, Americans have found barriers that they usually do not encounter in the United States. For example, the common American practice of cold-calling executives at high-tech firms for possible investment leads hasn't worked well in Europe, reflecting the common reluctance among Europeans of sharing information with strangers. American VCs have been pressing ahead anyway, but the learning process can be slow and costly.

As we have seen, Atila places a great deal of emphasis on exit, or what is sometimes known as "harvesting"—that is, how and when the company will cash out and realize its return. Going public and the private sale of the venture to another firm are the two alternatives that normally receive the most attention in business plans, but other approaches are more common.[6] These include buyouts by managers of the venture or members of the VC team, management buy-ins (in which the firm is bought by a group of outside investors who will then manage it), and collection of the ongoing free cash flow of the business over time.

Atila, like most VC firms, is privately owned. There are, however, publicly traded vehicles that permit the general investing public to participate in the venture capital business. One of the best known examples is 3i, the United Kingdom's largest private equity investor. This firm receives thousands of proposals each year and invests in several hundred of them. About half of its portfolio is composed of investments made in the prior three years, but unlike Atila, investments are not normally made with a fixed exit in mind. In contrast to most other VC firms, 3i prefers investments that produce at least some income during their lives in addition to any profit the company will get upon exit. The publicly listed status of 3i, and thus its desire to pay a dividend, apparently has some influence on this policy. Also, given the large number of companies in 3i's portfolio, it is typically less involved in the active management of the ventures in which it invests, in contrast to smaller VC firms.

Like Atila, 3i tends to favor established companies that need capital to finance expansion, although it does invest in start-ups, too. But while Atila often co-invests with other VCs, 3i is typically the sole investor in its transactions. The firm's large capital base, and the constant inflow of funds made available by exiting older investments, means that 3i can make deals on a scale far greater than any midsize firm such at Atila. In fact, 3i has done single deals involving amounts far exceeding the value of Atila's entire portfolio.

One important recent trend in private equity is the growth of corporate involvement. Siemens, the large diversified German engineering company, is a good example. It now has a venture capital unit that invests in selected technologies, especially software, that have applications in Siemens businesses. Reuters and Bertelsmann also have well-funded VC units. In fact, roughly half of the 100 largest firms in the United Kingdom have corporate venturing arms. As for the United States, Oracle is a prominent example. One of the motives for such corporate involvement is to help the business keep tabs on developments in new technology and their likely impact. Nearly always, this is done by investing in early-stage ventures in their own industry. The Dutch giant Royal Philips Electronics has used its venture fund to leapfrog its own research and development, which had become slow and bureaucracy laden. In essence, the venturing is a way of outsourcing some of the company's R&D, with the aim of more quickly identifying promising new markets and products.

The verdict on corporate venturing is decidedly mixed. Several companies even abandoned the practice after the dot-com meltdown. British Petroleum, however, has an enviable track record, posting annual returns in excess of 30 percent. Perhaps the most important lesson learned from these experiences, good and bad, is that those ventures that are closely linked to the company's core strategy are most likely to succeed.

Regardless of the size or nature of the venture capital firm, an important feature of VC finance is that investments are typically made in stages. In other words, when entrepreneurs receive commitments for investment funds, the funds are not normally invested up front as a lump sum. Rather, they are staged and linked to achieving specific milestones. Financing one stage does not commit the VC to finance later stages. The staging of investments reflects the commonsense idea that investors should wait and see before making a total commitment to the venture. In effect, the VCs ration small amounts of cash in the early stages, with further support contingent on the venture hitting a series of financial targets. Sometimes VCs—and angels, too—use the first round of financing mainly to begin the relationship with an entrepreneur, with more substantial funding, and more structured deals, coming in a later round. In addition, as Atila's experience shows, the source of financing of a particular venture often is different at each stage, reflecting the different risk-taking propensities and talents of different investors. Most of Atila's investments are made beyond the seed capital phase, either in late start-up or early expansion. Some VC firms, and most angels, focus their attention on less seasoned businesses.

The nature of the milestones, or what some VCs call "value events," depends on the stage of development. But in all cases, milestones are specific and verifiable performance benchmarks. They typically signal an important event or transition in the life of the business, one that might go some way in reducing risk and helping the company reach the next level of development and financing. Very simply, outside investors want to see tangible evidence that both reduces uncertainty about the market potential of the business model and reveals the entrepreneur's abilities.

For early-stage investments, especially those that are still considered start-ups, the first sale can be an important milestone. (Investors should take care to ensure that the sale is genuinely arm's-length; some unscrupulous entrepreneurs have created the illusion of sales by transacting with affiliated businesses.) Evidence of repeat sales is another example. So, too, is the hiring of a professional management team. Producing a prototype and completing the first production run are also important value events. After the first run, evidence of the company's ability to scale up production is another value event. In the retail sector, launching a store—or even better, rolling out a second store—can be a key event.

One way to think about these events is that they represent what must happen in the business to make it attractive to later-stage investors. For example, a value event to an angel investor is any important milestone that increases the chances of bringing in VC finance. To the venture capitalist, a value event would include key milestones that prepare the company for later-stage VC finance or for a public offering.

The recent collapse of technology and Internet stocks has, if anything, magnified the importance of milestones and performance targets. Since the crash and the huge losses suffered by some VCs, financing, when it does become available, comes on very tough terms. Strict goals are set and must be met if additional funds are to be meted out. Some VCs are even demanding a "liquidation preference," in which they get a guaranteed return in the event of a sale or public flotation, before the founding entrepreneur gets anything.

VCs have also become more careful about bringing their investments to market. Before the Internet boom, start-ups usually required years of seasoning before they were deemed ready for an IPO. But the Netscape IPO in August 1995 changed everything. Public equity investors suddenly seemed willing to invest in businesses that had yet to earn a profit, and might never do so. The result was not just an explosion in venture capital, but the speculative bubble that gripped Nasdaq until it all came crashing down in March 2000.

There is no clear line of demarcation between the expansion phase and the next stage of a firm's development, but one common boundary is the initial public offering. The IPO is a defining event in the life of any business, in terms of operations, size, and financing.

The most obvious advantage of going public is that it opens up new avenues for acquiring capital. Private firms are restricted in their access to external financing, both for debt and for equity. The access to new capital is especially important for high-growth businesses with large, profitable investment opportunities. A secondary benefit is that previous owners, such as venture capitalists and angel investors, can use the public offering to cash out. However, there are other consequences to being a publicly traded firm, and whether their influence is positive or negative depends largely on one's perspective. For example, corporate control issues arise. As companies get bigger, and the owners gradually sell off some of their shares, control might pass to other shareholders. Conflicts among these shareholder groups may be the result. One of the most famous examples of such conflict occurred when co-founder Steve Jobs was forced out at Apple Computer by the man he had recruited to run it.[7]

39

There are also legal and disclosure issues to ponder when going public. When companies are publicly traded, reams of financial data must be released on a regular basis to the general public. A company that runs afoul of securities regulations can become the target for lawsuits from agencies such as the Securities and Exchange Commission and from shareholders. Extensive public disclosure requirements may also force companies to reveal information about their operations that they would rather keep secret for competitive reasons. Also, a public listing requires management to spend a significant portion of its time on investor relations. In fact, some chief financial officers are in almost daily contact with the analyst community. And finally, public offerings are not possible without the help of investment bankers, and their services do not come cheap.

Overall, while the costs of going public can be substantial, for firms with large growth prospects and the need to finance them the net benefits to going public should be substantial. For firms with smaller growth opportunities, or with enough internally generated cash flows to finance investment, going public is less attractive. Cargill, Inc., is an example of a firm in the latter category. The company has managed to remain private and raise enough capital through internal resources and bank debt to grow at healthy rates for a long time.

A further complicating factor in public offerings is that the market never really seems to be in equilibrium. It's either too hot, as it was during the dot-com boom, or too cold, as it was after March 2000, when the dot-com craze fizzled. One way for managers to ensure that their company enjoys the benefits available from a public listing is to thoroughly plan for the support of the company's stock when it begins trading in the aftermarket (i.e., after the IPO takes place). This means understanding how the company will be positioned in relation to the market and to its industry competitors. It also requires knowledge of the analyst community, including who is likely to cover the stock and how the company should communicate with analysts to get across the value-creating potential of its business.

Once the decision to go public has been made, a business cannot approach the capital markets on its own. Because the firm is largely unknown to investors and it lacks the expertise to manage the intricacies of a public offering, it must choose a financial intermediary, usually an investment banker, to facilitate the transaction. Investment bankers offer the access to investors and the specialized knowledge of filing the necessary registration documents that the business itself does not have. They have expertise on markets and valuation to advise the company on the pricing of the new issue.

But perhaps the most important benefit afforded by investment bankers is that they can absorb some of the pricing risk of the issue by offering an underwriting guarantee. In essence, the bank creates a syndicate of banks that buy the new issue at a specific price (thus guaranteeing a certain level of proceeds to the issuing company). The members of the syndicate then use their sales forces to place the shares with clients. The difference between the price paid by clients for the new shares and the proceeds received by the issuing business represents the underwriters' commission. For the largest IPOs (i.e., those in excess of $100 million), commissions of slightly less than 4 percent of the total size of the issue are the norm. This percentage increases as the size of the offering decreases, rising to nearly 6 percent or even more for issues of under $10 million. Legal and administrative costs, including filing fees and the costs of preparing registration statements, can also be an important consideration, especially for relatively small offerings. But for any offering greater than, say, $25 million, these costs, while significant in absolute terms, are modest as a percentage of the total.

In setting the offering price (that is, the price that investors will be asked to pay for each share of stock), the investment bankers must first check investor demand. They do this through a process called "building the book," in which investors, mainly from financial institutions (such as mutual funds and insurance companies), are polled to gauge the extent of demand for the issue. To build demand, investment bankers organize a series of presentations, known as "road shows," to present information about the company to these prospective investors. The idea is to visit key financial centers where significant numbers of portfolio managers can be found—obvious examples being New York, Boston, London, Chicago, and Toronto. Senior managers from the issuing company accompany the bankers to present their company and to answer questions.

## Post-IPO Growth

In the typical post-IPO growth company, revenues and operating cash flows may be increasing and the profitability of the business may have been firmly established, but investment needs usually outstrip internally generated resources. In other words, while operating cash flows may be positive and growing, *free* cash flows are negative. In such cases, the company needs more external funding. There are exceptions, of course. Some firms, such as Microsoft, stay in a high growth phase for a long period without need for external financing because of extraordinary high profitability and free cash flows. But such companies are the exception, and not the rule.

The increase in equity funding, liquidity, investor interest, and size brought on by a public equity offering sometimes makes companies good candidates for other forms of financing not normally available to smaller firms. For example, access to corporate bond markets becomes a real possibility, offering the company an opportunity to access a broad pool of capital at a lower cost than it would pay to bankers for the same level of financing.

In short, as a company goes from being private to public, it finds itself with the visibility that enhances its access to other sources of capital. The history of Amazon.com is a classic example of how a company passes through the various stages of financing, and once it turns public can access a source of financing previously closed to it. Starting in mid-1994 with $10,000 of investment from its founder, Jeff Bezos, and a $44,000 loan, the company then raised $245,000 in the first half of 1995 from the founder's parents. Later that year, and stretching through 1996, angels contributed a total of about $1 million. In June 1996 the company took in $8 million from two venture capital funds. An initial public offering in the following year raised another $49.1 million. Then, in the first half of 1998, the company collected $236 million from a bond issue, using about one-third of it to retire previous loans, and the rest to finance operations. In short, Amazon went from bootstrapping to angel financing, then to venture capital and a public equity offering. After the IPO, it raised additional capital through a public debt issue.

In addition to corporate bonds, the company can raise capital by issuing warrants (a type of stock option) or new shares. New shares can be issued through a general subscription, in which the shares are available to the general investing public; a private placement, in which shares are sold directly to large investors; and rights offerings, in which shares are offered only to existing shareholders, usually at a bargain price. Each approach has its relative advantages and disadvantages.

For example, a general subscription accesses the broadest group of investors, but is also the most expensive way to raise additional equity (because of high investment banking fees). Private placements are much cheaper because they bypass the underwriting and marketing costs of investment bankers (terms are negotiated directly between the issuing company and the investor), and the administrative costs of filing the issue are lower, too; but the number of potential investors is small. One reason for the reluctance of investors, even very large ones, to invest in private placements of equity is that their portfolios may then be too heavily skewed to one company. This risk is of less concern for debt issues, which is why private placements are far more common for corporate bonds. Like private placements, rights offerings are a low-cost way to raise equity capital and are popular with shareholders, but they do not expand the investor base of the company. Many finance professionals believe that by expanding that base, a company can reduce its cost of capital.

## Low Growth and Maturity

A question often asked by managers of large, successful companies is, "Why should we care about capital markets when we have all the capital we need for current and future investment?" The question is motivated by the observation that the company generates more than sufficient cash flows from its business to finance any capital investment opportunity. Even if a company does not need to access additional external capital resources, and therefore does not require additional loans or equity capital, it should always be kept in mind that the company still has shareholders.

When companies generate surplus cash from their activities, there are choices for managers to make. Do we invest this surplus cash or do we return it to shareholders? The cash should be invested if managers believe that the invested funds will earn a return for shareholders greater than what they would expect to get if they were given the cash and had to invest it themselves. If the invested cash can earn these "supernormal" returns, shareholders would prefer that the company keep the cash and invest it on their behalf. But even in such cases, management still has the obligation to communicate the value-creating potential of these investments to the capital markets. Otherwise, investors might conclude that company resources are being squandered and value is being destroyed. When that happens, share price can only go down. If the magnitude of the share price decline is big enough, the company might even become a target for takeover. Remember, too, that if stock price has declined because of poor investments in the past, shareholders are less likely to trust managers to reinvest their cash flows for them in the future. In short, capital markets still matter, even for companies that don't need to raise any more capital.

As we noted earlier, the quality of a venture's management team plays a vital role for venture capitalists in deciding where to invest. The quality of management may be even more critical to the attractiveness of a mature, publicly traded company. For example, much of the allure of General Electric in the 1990s, which helped to push its value into the hundreds of billions of dollars, was the confidence that investors had in the company's chief executive, Jack Welch. Given that value is ultimately driven by capital market expectations of the future, the importance placed on top managers is hardly surprising. By their willingness to pay a high price for GE's stock, investors were signaling their beliefs that Welch and his management team were uniquely positioned to capture the value-creating potential of their business.

## Decline

At this stage, revenues, profits, and cash flows start to decline, but the company may still produce positive cash flows. Given that investment needs are modest, normally limited to replacing retired assets, internally generated resources are likely to exceed investment. Therefore, the firm probably has no need for external financing, whether equity or debt. In fact, it is more likely to retire existing debt and buy back shares. Firms in this phase don't take in capital; they give it back. Simply put, such businesses gradually liquidate themselves.

The decline phase does not have to be seen as the depressing end to a process of business development, and there are plenty of examples of companies that have reinvented themselves after sustained periods of decline, providing patient investors with high returns. What is important is to recognize that the financing strategy of a firm must be continuously reviewed and changed as the company moves from growth through maturity and then into decline.

One common strategy for firms in decline is to reduce the need for capital by seeking to convert fixed costs into costs of a more variable nature. For example, contracts with suppliers or employees can be placed on a short-term basis, allowing the company to avoid having to incur costs on capacity it can't use. This strategy broadly resembles the bootstrapping approach we discussed earlier in the context of start-up businesses. In both cases, the continued operation of the firm depends on its ability to keep capital requirements, at least in the near future, as low as possible. In a sense, the declining firm has come full circle, imitating some aspects of behavior from its early, bootstrapping days.

There are many other strategies firms employ to stave off collapse, but not all of them are beneficial to investors, a fact well known to capital market professionals. One obvious strategy is to diversify into other businesses, presumably with greater growth potential. But if managers have no special expertise that would allow the firm to add value in these growth sectors, the diversification move will almost certainly destroy shareholder value. It is widely understood that when managers pursue such strategies, it is often more to advance their own agendas than to make their shareholders better off. That's why the stock market's reaction to such efforts is nearly always negative.

An "industry roll-up" is a more attractive strategy. When companies are in decline, it's often because their industry is in decline too, which means that other firms face a similar fate. But while several relatively small or medium-sized firms might not make a go of it, a smaller number of large firms might. By selling off all nonessential assets, a firm might be able to raise the resources it needs to "roll up" its smaller competitors, in the process creating a larger, financially stronger business.

Once the firm has achieved a stronger market share, it may be able to improve financial performance dramatically by rationalizing the total capacity of the newly formed group. The effect is to remove some of the industry's excess capacity, which in turn should relieve some of the pressure on prices. Also, greater market share may give the business more leverage with suppliers and customers, thus increasing its share of the profits in the industry's value chain. What this approach illustrates is that the industry may not have been in decline after all. Instead, the problem may have been caused by unfortunate industry dynamics that had been allowed to develop. The result is that several small, declining businesses are transformed into one or two larger ones that may actually have a promising future.

## OTHER INFLUENCES ON FINANCING

Although a firm's stage of development is the single biggest influence on its financing choices, there are other considerations as well. For example, the urgency of a company's financing needs will often dictate how funds are raised. If a venture faces an immediate need for financing, many sources are impractical, if not impossible. Generally, the opportunity to raise additional equity is foreclosed, unless the entrepreneur has an established relationship with an equity investor. But even in such cases, quick injections of capital are hard to get. Angel investor groups, and especially venture capital firms, often have lengthy due diligence and internal approval processes.

For publicly traded companies, selling equity to passive investors may be an option, but a registered public offering of equity takes at least several weeks, if not months, to complete. One alternative available to such firms is to reissue shares held in corporate treasury (that is, resell shares that had been previously bought back from shareholders). This is a popular, low-cost, and quick way to raise equity capital, although the amounts that companies can raise through this method generally fall far short of what they can raise through public offerings.

For many firms, both private and publicly traded, the most realistic sources of immediate financing are those for which no negotiation or approval process is required or for which financing is preapproved. Usually, this involves some form of bank debt, such as a line of credit. The obvious problem for small ventures, however, is that banks are often reluctant to extend unsecured lines of credit to high-risk companies, and if they do, the credit lines are capped at low levels that are unlikely to suffice in a crunch. In any event, raising finance in a crisis is nearly always expensive.

When financing needs are of a less immediate nature, more alternatives become available. This is true for all types of businesses. Equity capital becomes a more realistic possibility, perhaps in the form of private placements with wealthy investors or with large institutions such as pension funds and insurance companies, or through a registered public offering.

Income taxes and bankruptcy costs are other important influences over financing choices. The Nobel Prize–winning insights of Franco Modigliani and Merton Miller shed light on why these factors matter. Although debt finance is cheaper than equity, they showed that, in a world without taxes and without bankruptcy costs, the benefit from substituting cheaper debt for expensive equity is exactly offset by higher risk (and correspondingly higher cost) for the remaining equity. The result is that the company's *weighted average* cost of capital is unaffected by the financing choice, and so, too, is its value.

Of course, in the real world we have both taxes and bankruptcy costs. And because the interest companies pay to their bankers and bondholders is tax deductible, debt affords valuable advantages. In other words, debt can, up to a point, reduce a company's cost of capital and thus create value. This is why highly profitable companies, such as Coca-Cola and Merck, have debt in their capital structures even though they don't really need the debt capital to finance their investments. Both companies are more than capable of financing all of their investment needs from internally generated cash flows. But like all profitable firms, their taxes loom large. In a sense, by forcing themselves to take on debt and to keep it on their balance sheets, they get a tax deduction, or tax shield, that can protect some of their operating profits from tax.

But the more debt a company takes on, the greater the risk that it will be unable to service that debt should bad things happen, such as economic slowdowns or the loss of major customers. This risk carries real costs to companies, both direct (e.g., the fees that must be paid to lawyers, investment bankers, and accountants should the company be forced to undergo financial restructuring) and indirect (e.g., lost sales and declining employee morale). Therefore, financing choice requires a delicate balancing act, in which the benefits of a valuable tax shield from debt are offset against the costs brought on by higher bankruptcy risk.

## A SPECIAL CASE:
## FINANCIALLY TROUBLED FIRMS

The threat of bankruptcy brings to mind the challenge of raising capital for firms in financial distress. At first glance, because of the high risk involved, the financing of distressed firms bears a strong resemblance to the financing of high-risk start-ups. But there are important differences. Financial distress means the entrepreneur already has failed to achieve a level of success consistent with expectations. That failure can undermine the entrepreneur's credibility in the eyes of investors. The entrepreneur of a start-up may present considerable risk to investors, but at least does not suffer from the taint of failure.

A venture may get into trouble because of strategic issues, poor management, or financial planning and control problems. Strategic issues include misperceiving the market opportunity or selecting an organizational design that doesn't work for that business. Management issues arise because the company lacks critical skills or loses too many key people. Financial planning and control problems can lead to unexpected cash shortages, and may be caused by poor pricing decisions and runaway costs.

Although any new venture may encounter such problems, a financially distressed business already has. In a sense, the question mark that hangs over any venture has been answered, but not in a way that is flattering to the entrepreneur or to the management team. Given that the venture has failed, or is on the verge of failing, why should investors assume that projections in a revised plan are achievable or that existing management is capable of turning things around?

The financial structure of most firms is based on a premise that the venture will be successful. Creditors, including suppliers and even employees, expect that they will be paid what is owed to them. But when a venture gets into financial trouble, creditors' perspectives change. Secured creditors look more intently at the value of collateral as a source of repayment. Their concern is that if the entrepreneur is allowed to continue operating the business, the collateral may depreciate. They may press for liquidation of the collateral as a means of repayment. This situation may create conflicts with other capital providers, such as unsecured creditors (i.e., those without collateral to back up their loans), who figure that they are not likely to see much cash if the company is forced to liquidate. They usually prefer that the company will continue to operate, in the hope that a turnaround may follow.

Meanwhile, suppliers to financially distressed firms no longer assume that they will be paid. They may demand cash payment. Because the venture's tight cash situation probably makes this impossible, the company runs the very considerable risk of seeing its supply chain disrupted. The result is that the company digs itself into an even deeper financial hole. For their part, employees may assume that their jobs are at risk and may try to protect themselves by seeking new employment.

Even customers may become concerned and stop purchasing. This risk is especially high in industries where product warranties, after-sales service, or safety are primary concerns to the buyer. Baan NV, a large Dutch software company, faced this problem when it reported large losses in 1999. Once one of Europe's high-tech success stories, the company suffered through declining sales, departing executives, and accounting scandals. The result was a loss in confidence in it by large corporate customers. Without such confidence, customers could not be sure that the company would be around to maintain and upgrade the software.[8]

Turning around a distressed firm can be more difficult than raising initial financing for a risky venture. One reason for this is because the financing is already in place and the threat of financial distress creates conflicts among the various stakeholders. These conflicts extend beyond those of secured and unsecured creditors, as discussed earlier. The conflict between bankers and other providers of debt finance on one hand and equity investors on the other is potentially even more devastating. When companies get into serious financial trouble, the temptation for owners/entrepreneurs may be to adopt excessively risky operating strategies in much the same way that struggling gamblers might put all of their dwindling resources on one more roll of the dice. Double or nothing. If they win, they keep playing. Even if they lose, they reckon that they would probably have lost anyway. Of course, lenders know this might happen, which makes the raising of the capital needed to save the business that much harder.

The objective in turnaround finance is clear enough: To devise a new capital structure for the firm such that each party expects to be better off by maintaining or increasing its investment than by collecting the liquidation value of its financial claims. But even if it is apparent that the going-concern value exceeds the liquidation value, financial restructuring is never easy.

## CONCLUSIONS

Nearly all investors seek the highest risk-return profile on their capital, regardless of whether they invest in early-stage ventures or large, established publicly traded companies. But the criteria used to analyze investment opportunities, and determine where capital resources can be best deployed, depend on the stage of the investment. In other words, what matters most to investors will change as companies pass through the life cycle.

## NOTES

1. Bruce W. Marcus and Sherwood Lee Wallace, *New Dimensions in Investor Relations: Competing for Capital in the 21st Century*, New York: John Wiley & Sons, 1997, p. 8.
2. Mark Van Osnabrugge and Robert J. Robinson, *Angel Investing: Matching Start-up Funds with Start-up Companies*, San Francisco: Jossey-Bass, 2000, p. 5.
3. Ibid., p. 8.
4. David Amis and Howard Stevenson, *Winning Angels: The 7 Fundamentals of Early Stage Investing*, London: Financial Times/Prentice Hall, 2001, pp. 12–13.
5. Van Osnabrugge and Robinson, *Angel Investing*, p. 123.
6. Ibid., p. 567.
7. Years later, Jobs returned as Apple's CEO and engineered an impressive turnaround in the company's fortunes.
8. S. David Young and Stephen F. O'Byrne, *EVA and Value-Based Management: A Practical Guide to Implementation*, New York: McGraw-Hill, 2001, p. 190.

PART TWO

# UNDERSTANDING INVESTORS AND LENDERS

# 3

# Early-Stage Financing: The Role of Business Angels

WHAT IS AN ANGEL?

WHERE DO ANGELS GET THEIR INVESTMENT
  IDEAS?

WHAT MOTIVATES THE ANGEL INVESTOR?

TYPES OF ANGEL INVESTORS

HOW TO ATTRACT ANGELS

WHAT ANGELS ARE LOOKING FOR

In the preceding chapter, we showed that the most likely sources of capital for a particular business depend on its stage of development. For many businesses, financing follows a logical sequence, starting with personal savings and bootstrapping, as well as funding sources close to the entrepreneur (namely, family and friends). In this chapter, we explore the next link in the chain: business angels. Such investors are the major providers of equity finance for businesses that have moved beyond the bootstrapping, family and friends stage, but may not yet be ready for, or of interest to, venture capitalists. Angels are more likely than other types of investors to be the first truly external source of financing for a growing business. Angels fill the gap between family and friends, whose investments tend to be limited to the low five figures (in U.S. dollar terms) and venture capitalists, who generally invest in the high six figures and often far more. Although precise figures are hard to come by, anecdotal evidence suggests that the average investment by angels in the United States is between $100,000 and $150,000. Investments can run as high as $500,000, or even more when angels invest in groups.

Angel investing has always been around, but it really took off in the 1990s. Rising incomes and a bullish stock market created a pool of wealthy individuals looking for places to invest other than conventional securities such as stocks and bonds. Of course, with the post-dot-com meltdown and the resulting economic slowdown, the volume of angel financing worldwide has declined. But angel networks have emerged in every advanced market economy in the world, and even in some developing countries. And as economies recover, the amount of capital available from these investors recovers, too. Even during the economic slowdown in the United States in 2001 and 2002, tens of thousands of small businesses received at least some funding from angels.

## WHAT IS AN ANGEL?

Given the very nature of angel investing, there are no formal requirements to participate. Still, some observers have tried to define angels with at least some precision. Gerald A. Benjamin and Joel Margulis, in *The Angel Investor's Handbook: How to Profit from Early-Stage Investing,*[1] describe angels as wealthy individuals willing to invest in high-risk deals offered by entrepreneurs whom they admire and with whom they wish to be associated. Others have defined business angels as people who provide equity capital to companies without the intervention of a third party, such as a venture capital firm. To put it another way, angels invest directly, not through intermediaries.

Just about anyone can be an angel as long as they have sufficient personal wealth and a willingness to invest in high-risk ventures. But for many angels, it's not just about the money. Although money is always important for angels, they may also look for nonfinancial rewards from investing.

A good rule of thumb for whether someone is a good candidate for angel status, at least in the American context, is to draw on the standards set by the U.S. Securities and Exchange Commission (SEC) for "accredited" status under Regulation D. Currently such status requires a net worth of at least $1 million and an annual income of at least $200,000 (or $300,000 for married couples). It implies that the investor is rich enough to deal with the high risk of investing in equity stakes that cannot be readily bought and sold in public securities markets. Although the standard seems to severely restrict the number of potential investors in this market, robust economic growth in the 1980s and 1990s created a large pool of investors, in the United States and elsewhere, with the financial means and the inclination to participate.

Broadly speaking, angel investors are either passive or active. Whereas passive investors do not involve themselves in the operations of the businesses they invest in, active investors work in an advisory capacity, and in some cases (though not usually) may become involved in key operating decisions. Most angels have some experience as entrepreneurs. Two-thirds of angels in the United States have set up companies at least twice. Many of these angels, especially those who take active or advisory roles in investee firms, have worked in high-tech businesses or in financial services. This experience puts them in a strong position to help entrepreneurs in the management of their businesses.

Experience has shown that in the case of active angels, four factors are critical if the relationship with the entrepreneur is to be productive and mutually profitable. First, the angel should have industry knowledge and skills that the entrepreneur can use. Second, the angel should have contacts with suppliers, potential customers, and other relevant parties that can help the business to expand. Third, there must be good chemistry between investor and entrepreneur. Of course, personal chemistry is always important, but it is even more critical for active investors than for passive ones because of their direct involvement in the business. And finally, the entrepreneur should be "coachable," that is, responsive to the advice on offer from the investor.

## WHERE DO ANGELS GET THEIR INVESTMENT IDEAS?

Angels identify investment opportunities, or what is sometimes called "deal flow," in two principal ways: networking and visibility activities.[2] Networking includes meetings with bankers, lawyers, accountants, and others who come in contact with entrepreneurs in need of capital. Also, most major cities in the United States and several in Europe have angel groups where investors get together to discuss and sometimes collaborate on potential deals. Angel/entrepreneur matchmakers are another source of deal flow, with the special attraction to the investor of prescreening performed by the matchmaker. Venture capitalists, too, feed investment opportunities to angels, especially if they believe that the venture in question is not seasoned enough to justify VC investment but might be later. The hope is that the angels will then turn to the VCs when the time is right and a round of VC financing is called for.

Visibility activities include anything that angels might do to signal their intent to the general public, entrepreneurs, and other investors. In addition to making investments or co-investing with other angels, these activities include giving speeches, publishing articles, and granting interviews to the business press.[3]

Later in this chapter we discuss how entrepreneurs can get

on an angel's radar screen and increase the likelihood that they, too, can be part of the deal flow.

## WHAT MOTIVATES
## THE ANGEL INVESTOR?

Experience has shown that angels are driven by any one or more of these motives, although a seeker of angel finance would be well served to assume that the first of these motives is the most important:

- *Financial reward.* Angels invest with the prospect of a high financial reward. A good rule of thumb is that angels hope to quintuple their money in five years, although only a few actually do so. While financial criteria are rarely stated explicitly, they may be implicit in the investor's decision to commit to market niches with great growth potential. In general, angels place less weight than VCs and other professional investors on the financial projections presented by the entrepreneur. Instead, they rely on gut feeling that a particular entrepreneur is worth investing in. Still, there are angels, a minority to be sure but a sizable one, who take a more professional approach, and they will often have explicit annual return goals in mind. Typically, these return objectives range between 25 and 50 percent.
- *Playing a role in the entrepreneurial process.* Angels enjoy their involvement in an entrepreneurial process. Given that most such investors are in their forties or

fifties, and have already achieved success in their careers or with their own businesses, they like to use the time and money available to them to once again experience the thrill and challenge of nurturing a new business.

- *Altruism.* Although the term *angels* might give the impression that altruism is a motive, it is rarely the primary one. In some cases, however, investors are keen to pass on their skills to the next generation of entrepreneurs. Their hope is to encourage a spirit of entrepreneurship that can create jobs and promote economic prosperity. This motive tends to be more common among angels living in rural areas or in small towns.

## TYPES OF ANGEL INVESTORS

Given that there are hundreds of thousands of angels worldwide, at least a quarter-million of whom reside in the United States, with diverse motives and experiences, there is no such thing as a prototypical angel. Still, some broad conclusions can be drawn. Data compiled by the International Capital Resources, based on a survey of 1,200 investors in 1999 and 2000, shows most angel investors to be men between 46 and 65 years old. Many of these investors have postgraduate degrees and extensive business experience. Commonly, angels owned, and then sold, their own companies. Having had to raise money for their businesses, many have experience in dealing with investors. They understand the risks of early-stage investments, and also the potential for high returns.

Most angels prefer to invest close to home. However, recent research has shown that perhaps one-third of all angels believe that geographic proximity to the venture is not a major concern. What matters more is the need for the lead investor, whether another angel or some other party, to be close to the deal and that he or she is known and respected.[4]

Compared to venture capitalists, angels have a more flexible attitude toward the types of businesses they consider investing in. Also, because the amounts at stake are usually far smaller, they tend to move faster than VCs. About half of all angels need less than a month after first seeing the business plan to decide whether to invest. The due diligence process of the venture capitalist means that only rarely can deals be struck so quickly.

The background, interests, and industry specializations of angel investors vary widely, but most fall into one of the following categories (although it should be noted that some investors exhibit characteristics of two or more angel types, and that the nature of a particular angel's participation can vary from one investment to the next).

- *Entrepreneurial angels.* These investors are sometimes prepared to invest larger sums and take bigger risks than the average angel. Most own and operate a successful business, or have done so. Their investments can run as high as $500,000, but are often far less. Such angels diversify to avoid being overly dependent on any one investment. Most entrepreneurial angels insist on board representation, but normally do not interfere with the day-to-day management of the business.

64

- *Lifestyle angels.* Investors of this type consider investment mainly as a hobby. Generally they are not involved
  in managing the business or advising the entrepreneur,
  and thus take a passive role. Their investments can be as
  low as $10,000, but may run into the low six figures.

- *Profession-based angels.* These angels are linked to a
  profession such as medicine, law, or accounting, and
  prefer to invest in companies suited to their expertise
  and experience. Although they will not be too actively
  involved in the entrepreneurial process, they will share
  their capabilities and knowledge. Their investments usually range from around $25,000 to the low six figures.

- *Altruistic angels.* These investors are motivated both by
  financial profit and by the desire to do good. The Community Development Venture Capital Alliance, a nonprofit organization based in New York, is devoted to
  bringing together such investors with capital-seeking
  entrepreneurs.[5]

- *Alliance angels.* These angels invest in groups. Many
  such investors lack the necessary background to coach
  entrepreneurs, and thus tend to be passive, although an
  important subset does have relevant professional experience and thus tends to take on more active roles in the
  businesses they finance. One element that these angels
  have in common is that they seek to share risk with others or to participate in deals that would otherwise be
  too big for one investor. They sometimes operate
  through informal networks known as "angel alliances."
  These alliances usually hold meetings on a routine basis
  and, if interested in a particular proposal, will decide

quickly whether to invest. One of the better-known examples is the Band of Angels, based in Silicon Valley. Because it pools capital from lots of angels (more than 100 at last count), its average investment is over $500,000. This level of investment is similar to the smaller deals done by venture capitalists.

## HOW TO ATTRACT ANGELS

Before they can attract angel financing, entrepreneurs have to find them first. An obvious point, of course, but it reflects a fundamental difference between angels and other private equity investors. While there are undoubtedly many more angels than venture capitalists, angels are harder to locate. Unlike VCs, for example, angels generally don't advertise themselves. You won't find listings of them in phone books. By its very nature, angel investing tends to be ad hoc and informal.

A good place to start looking is among family and friends. Indeed, angel investing can sometimes be a logical extension of such financing. Advertising campaigns are out of the question, because such activities are forbidden in most countries. In the United States, for example, the Securities and Exchange Commission forbids general advertising and solicitation for investors in privately held companies. Placing ads in business periodicals is clearly not allowed. If angels are to be found, it must be through some other approach.

Networking at trade shows and industry events is one popular way of getting to know potential investors. Local business associations offer similar attractions. Angel clubs, bringing together like-minded investors, have emerged in several large

U.S. cities, and in some European capitals as well. They typically meet once a month, often in the offices of a local bank or investment firm.

Web-based services can also be fruitful. One prominent example in the United States is ACE-Net, or the Angel Capital Electronic Network. Through its web site (www.ace-net.org) and several local networking organizations, it aims to bring entrepreneurs in direct contact with angels and other private equity investors. Capital seekers post business plans online, allowing potential funders to respond if interested. This initiative was sponsored by the Small Business Administration, and has attracted a host of imitators.

Many deals between angels and entrepreneurs have been struck as the result of such services, but there are two significant drawbacks to consider. One of these drawbacks is the potential loss of confidentiality. Although ACE-Net and similar services try to preserve confidentiality, the audience may be comprised of potential competitors. And where there are potential competitors, there is always the possibility that valuable, proprietary business ideas will be stolen. A second concern, at least in the United States, is that postings on the Internet can, if not properly structured, run afoul of regulations on general solicitation. To avoid trouble, the sponsors of these web sites try to ensure that only investors that satisfy the accreditation standards of the SEC are authorized to access the offerings posted on the Web, and that access is password protected. Reputable sponsors understand these rules and are quite scrupulous in adhering to them. Other operators might not be so careful.

Although all of these approaches play a useful role, one simple, uncomfortable fact remains. Despite the avenues for bringing entrepreneurs and angel investors together, the market is a relatively inefficient one, especially compared to more sophisticated forms of capital raising, such as venture capital and public offerings. There is no central clearinghouse providing information on size or pricing of recent deals. And while entrepreneurs often struggle to find interested angels, for their part, angels often struggle to find suitable deals. Yes, it's getting better, thanks partly to the Internet. But informational inefficiencies abound in this market. For this reason, it is widely accepted in the angel community that a lot of good deals never get funded simply because entrepreneur and angel never connect.

## WHAT ANGELS ARE LOOKING FOR

Entrepreneurs need to understand which aspects of their proposed business will carry the most weight in the decision of angels to invest. Here are the major questions that angels ask.

- *Does the entrepreneur inspire confidence?* Angels place considerable weight on the quality of the entrepreneur.[6] A business is run by people and if the people are wrong, the business will fail. Entrepreneurs must convince angels that they have both an entrepreneurial capability and a team with sound management skills. These entrepreneurs must also have a good educational background and a track record of performance in the business line of their choice. They must have great enthusiasm or passion for the business they are starting. The entrepreneur must put together a solid management team to give confidence that the various business activities can be run well.

- *What is the funding to be used for?* Given that angels tend to fund early-stage ventures, they strongly prefer that their investment goes directly into the company being capitalized. Although there are exceptions to this rule, investors normally exit after the angel stage of finance.

- *Does the venture fit with the angel's own investment profile?* This is why it is so important for capital-seeking entrepreneurs to target their pitches. There is little point in going after angels who don't invest in the venture's industry or whose risk profiles don't match the business. Prior to approaching angel investors, entrepreneurs should first understand their particular characteristics. What factors motivate the angels to invest, and what industrial sectors are attractive to them? They must be able to show how their business opportunity matches the angels' goals.

- *Does the business have genuine growth potential?* Entrepreneurs need to show that the business can take off. The business must have some unique characteristics that are likely to win customers against competition in the chosen market niche.[7] Is the venture doing something unique, and if so, is that something not easy for potential competitors to copy? Is the market big enough to make growth and cash flow projections possible?

  Also, most angels are wary of single-product businesses. They like focus, but can the business develop multiple income flows? This is not to say that single-product companies are unworthy of investment, but when revenue streams are dependent on one product, potential investors get nervous.

- **_Is there a credible business plan?_** Most angels want to see a business plan before investing.[8] A good plan will discuss the vision and mission of the company, and will also show financial projections, a marketing plan, a sales plan, and an outline of major operating controls.[9] At this stage, the plan should be short, concise, and to the point. It should summarize the products to be sold, the credentials of the management team, the financing sought and the reasons for seeking capital, any achievements of the venture to date, expected milestones, and exit strategies.[10]

## NOTES

1. Gerald A. Benjamin and Joel Margulis, *The Angel Investor's Handbook: How to Profit from Early-Stage Investing*, Princeton: Bloomberg Press, 2001.
2. David Amis and Howard Stevenson, *Winning Angels: The 7 Fundamentals of Early Stage Investing*, London: Financial Times/Prentice Hall, 2001, p. 36.
3. Ibid.
4. Benjamin and Margulis, *Angel Investor's Handbook*, pp. 32–34.
5. www.cdvca.org.
6. Mark Van Osnabrugge and Robert J. Robinson, *Angel Investing: Matching Start-up Funds with Start-up Companies*, San Francisco: Jossey-Bass, 2000, p. 123.

7. C. M. Mason and A. Rogers, "Understanding the Business Angel's Investment Decision." *Venture Finance Research Project*. (Working paper.) University of Southampton and Ulster Business School, Southampton, U.K., 1996.

8. C. M. Mason and R.T. Harrison, "The UK Clearing Banks and the Informal Venture Capital Market," *International Journal of Bank Marketing* 14(1), 1996, pp. 5–14.

9. Ibid.; R. H. Keeley, J. B. Roure, and R. Loo, "New Ventures Which Obtain Funding and Those Which Do Not: What's the Difference?" In *Frontiers of Entrepreneurship Research*, Babson Park, MA: Babson College, 1991.

10. S. Nance-Nash, "Brevity, Bullets and No B.S.," *Forbes*, February 18, 1999.

# 4

# Private Equity: Unleashing Your Company's Potential Value

OVERVIEW OF THE VENTURE CAPITAL PROCESS

THE WAY VENTURE CAPITALISTS WORK

THE FUNDING PROCESS
> Initial Meetings
> Due Diligence
> Negotiations
> The Closing

THE MOTIVATION OF VENTURE CAPITALISTS
> High Return on Investment
> Self-Actualization

GOING INTO BATTLE: HOW TO WIN OVER VENTURE CAPITALISTS
> Choose the Right One
> Get a Referral

M any entrepreneurs have visions of taking their firms public. Perhaps more than any other milestone in the life of a business, a public offering announces, "We have arrived." However, as we explore in the next chapter, raising capital through a public offering is not easy. The process is costly, and only firms that satisfy a strict set of criteria are likely to benefit. Other businesses, and this describes the overwhelming majority of entrepreneurial ventures, are far better served by seeking capital from a small number of individuals or organizations, and not the general investing public. That's what private equity offerings are for. In this chapter, we consider how funds can be obtained from firms that specialize in providing private equity finance. Most of our attention is focused on venture capital, because that's where most private equity comes from, but we also explore the important phenomenon of leveraged buyouts.

Venture capital (VC) can be defined as a long-term, equity-based investment to fuel the growth of young, privately held companies. Defined in still simpler terms, it is money invested in new companies, especially those touting new ideas or new forms of business.[1] Venture capital has also been described as illiquid, long-term investments in young and innovative ventures where both the risks and the potential returns are high. Most of these investments are made by VC firms that manage capital pooled from institutions and high-net-worth individuals. This practice contrasts sharply with that of business angels, who invest their own funds. Another important feature of VC financing, one it shares with angel financing, especially for early-stage investments, is that most ventures being funded have yet to show a profit.

## OVERVIEW OF THE VENTURE CAPITAL PROCESS

The primary reward for the providers of venture capital is capital gain, rather than interest income or dividend yield.[2] Venture capital firms may be the most likely source of external equity funding for the small percentage of entrepreneurial firms that survive the start-up phase and climb into high growth. However, VC funding can be hard to get, even for promising businesses. Entrepreneurial firms are risky, a reality that is further aggravated by the difficulty in evaluating the soft assets and real (i.e., strategic) options that are common to entrepreneurial companies.

Venture capitalists often act as funnels, acquiring funds from big companies and institutions and then distributing them to a group of carefully selected growing businesses. The venture company managers, or general partners, raise this money from pension funds, insurance companies, university endowments, corporations, foundations, wealthy individual investors, and government agencies.

Venture capitalists are a select group of people with investment management experience and a thorough knowledge of the early life cycles of companies. They can assist clients to develop a sustainable company, help to set up a distribution network, and overcome whatever challenges arise. They take an active involvement in, but do not run, the company. Instead, they serve as coaches for clients until exit (such as an initial public offering).

Venture capital investors come from a variety of backgrounds, bringing with them a range of experiences, attitudes, and business philosophies. Perhaps the most common image of a venture capitalist is of a middle-aged man with a strong financial background, but most venture capitalists are relatively young (under 50), and their field of expertise may lie outside finance, in marketing or technology, for example. Often, they come from the industries they invest in, having served in important operating roles; many are even ex-CEOs. One of the key trends in recent years has been the growing importance of such operating people, in contrast to the 1980s when finance specialists tended to dominate the industry.

To help smooth the way to funding, the entrepreneur has to understand what drives each venture capitalist to invest. Only then can the entrepreneur hope to be able to choose the type of venture capitalist that is in line with his or her business. Entrepreneurs seeking venture capital must propose solid business plans describing a high-potential market opportunity and detailing the steps to set up a business that can satisfy that demand in a profitable way. Referrals from sources trusted by the venture capitalist will also help to inspire confidence. The most important factor in determining whether to go ahead with the investment is the quality of the venture's people, in terms of leadership, vision, integrity, openness, and dedication. The background and experience of the potential investee's management team are also closely examined by the venture capitalists.

## THE WAY VENTURE CAPITALISTS WORK

Unfortunately for many start-ups, most venture capitalists are interested in funding projects seeking anywhere from $5 million to $20 million. Smaller projects do not appeal to them, owing to the high cost of investigation and administration. Fortunately for the young entrepreneur, the venture capital industry offers a range of specialist VCs, from seed capital to mezzanine. Proposals submitted by smaller projects might therefore be considered by seed and early-stage venture capitalists as long as the projects combine a strong management team, sound market opportunities, and a credible business model, and thus swift growth potential. Around 90 percent of all proposals will be rejected quickly because investors feel that they do not fit with their firm's geographical, industrial or technical policies, or because the business plans contained within the proposals do not match the criteria set by the investor firm and its charter. The bottom line is that although venture capitalists would logically be interested in any high-return project, they nonetheless choose to operate within a set of constraints.

When it is time to approach a venture capitalist, however, many entrepreneurs contribute to their own problems. Many simply lack a clear picture of the venture capital process or even of the entrepreneurial process that would minimize their own risk of failure. Venture capitalists complain that too many entrepreneurs try to launch a product or service that does not respond to an opportunity in the market. Also, they too often rely on naive analyses, business models, and marketing plans. Last but not least, the business plan and presentation materials are generally boring, undifferentiated, and, at times, sloppy. Even for the most motivated investor, it is hard not to stumble when confronted with a poorly written document. Risk needs to be reduced to make the proposal attractive to the venture capitalist. This risk is explained more fully in the sidebar.

---

## Inherent Risks in Venture Business

Venture capital investments promise high returns at moderate or high risk. Such a level of risk accompanies the inherent difficulties some borrowers have in winning financing, especially from traditional sources. Venture capital experts Professor Paul A. Gompers and Professor Josh Lerner of Harvard Business School identify four problem areas—volatile markets, perceived uncertainty differences, information gaps, and soft assets plus real options—that often frustrate entrepreneurial firms' money raising.

***Volatile Markets.*** The spring 2000 Nasdaq crash offers an interesting case study of a volatile market. Prior to the crash, many Internet companies had attracted massive valuations that then dived, meteorlike, in March and April. This dramatic change in their fortunes had a huge impact on these Internet companies. The severe market jolt meant companies were forced to deliver true value, while earlier growth-focused strategies, the previous trend, suddenly went out the window. Even top performers can have a tough time accessing funding if their sector becomes unpopular with public investors. In the past few years, the prevailing high market volatility has favored investments with a short payback, calling for compelling break-even analyses and "path to profitability" strategies.

A start-up's capacity to establish its market share, become profitable, and hence leverage its value, will also be severely challenged in such an unstable environment. This may then force these companies into an ever accelerating competition to enhance their products, in turn demanding large research and development outlays.

***Perceived Uncertainty Differences.*** It is a fact of life for all entrepreneurial companies that they must deal with an uncertain future, arising from market and industry trends, including competitor response and government/regulatory approvals, and also from how they tackle their own growth possibilities. This uncertainty can be looked at as how the company or project's possible outcomes are distributed. The greater the uncertainty, the wider the distribution of potential outcomes. Venture capitalists manage these uncertainties by assessing the most likely scenarios and the range of potential outcomes, and sometimes will even also determine an implementation schedule for the particular company to suit all these factors. Although all this may get written down, frequently it does not, as it is largely the result of intensive lengthy discussions within board and investment committees.

In venture capital, uncertainty is an aspect that affects all the key players: from suppliers' preparedness to extend a company credit, managers' choices of direction for their companies, and investors' willingness to invest. An investor and the entrepreneur may perceive these uncertainties differently; it is precisely this difference of perception that frequently turns this area into a source of major disagreements. Individuals inevitably have different ways of attempting to predict the future that involve their own attitudes, values, beliefs about themselves, and business. Entrepreneurs are generally convinced their start-up will succeed, while investors may want to hang back because they see more uncertainties. These indeterminate factors can be broadly categorized into two types. The first area of concern is the normal business risks that include management, technology, and markets. The second is investment risk. This is where an owner may set his asking price too high, making his company a poor investment.

***Information Gaps.*** All businesses' aspects are subject to information gaps. These are the differences between the essential information required for sound investment and what external parties already know about a company's internal workings, prospects, and market trends. When businesspersons and investors do not each have an in-depth knowledge and understanding of the other's environment, and are reluctant to disclose this missing detail for fear it would weaken their position, information gaps arise. Disputes between the two parties can then follow.

A businessperson, for instance, may want to keep the

perks and other benefits he gets as a manager of his own company and so decide to say nothing about some important issues. Alternatively, an entrepreneur may attempt to manipulate a company's performance reports to drive up its worth or to entice potential investors with a juicier proposal. As well, particularly early on in a company's history, an entrepreneur may not wish to divulge information because of concerns about potential loss of intellectual property.

These gaps may even lead an investor to pull out, thus worsening a company's situation by restricting access to further credit from suppliers and hampering its ability to take on new staff. What's more, information gaps markedly affect the types of financing investors make available and the corporate control they demand. In a worst-case scenario, a transaction that has the potential to benefit all parties may not happen, simply because of such information gaps.

***Soft Assets and Real Options.*** The real value of a business depends on its cash flows from its current assets plus the investment opportunities it can pursue in the future. There are two kinds of assets: the hard or physical kind, which include buildings, machinery, and real estate, and the soft or intangible ones, which include patents, trademarks, or the collective knowledge base of a company's human capital. The combined nature of all these assets determines a company's ability to raise funding and the conditions under which it is made available.

Companies with a preponderance of hard assets have more financing choices than those with soft ones, as hard assets are easier to value. Most hard assets have active secondary markets for resale, making it easy to set a value on them. The values of soft assets rarely get a mention in active market listings, because their value is so hard to estimate. Hence, soft assets have little attraction for prospective financiers as a basis for providing credit. Assets such as patents or new trademarks may have value if linked to other assets, or can be included, but marked down, as assets intrinsically tied to the company's overall value. Human capital can prove to be a valuable soft asset if a company can retain it. There is, too, generally very little choice in the asset structure of a business, as this depends on the particular industry.

Apart from soft assets, another source of value has been given considerable exposure recently. This is known as "real options," or future investment opportunities. A real option is essentially a derivative, closely resembling exchange-traded stock options (where the value of the financial instrument is *derived* from another asset); however, in real options the underlying asset offered is the business's growth potential. In short, it is a mathematical expression of the business's risk-return relationship. As with soft assets, real options prove difficult to quantify, because they are essentially an intangible projection of a company's ability to invest in new projects, the real success of which cannot ever be taken for granted. Accordingly, an investor would need to be thoroughly convinced about these future investment prospects before providing financing.

Adapted and reprinted by permission of the Havard Business School Press from *The Money of Invention* by Paul A. Gompers and Josh Lerner (Boston: Harvard Business School Press, 2001), pp. 21–40.

Venture capital firms are often deluged with proposals coming from entrepreneurs seeking funds. Most are passed over quickly. In the meantime, VCs are proactive in looking for good deals. Venture capital is a people business, and rarely do VCs consider deals that just happen to come through the door. As a first step, they usually look for disturbances in the market scene, to isolate specific industries that might offer high growth opportunities. They then zero in on these and start to actively get in the path of the flow. Several strategies can be set in place to create the expected deal flow, and almost all of them involve a trusted referral who recommends the deal. For instance, deals can be brought by existing portfolio companies' entrepreneurs and board members, as well as by attorneys and other professionals.

Specialized private equity consulting firms, such as the Grimaldi Group in New York, also offer deal generation services. They then act as an executive search firm would, but rather than seeking high-profile talent, they seek high-potential ventures that fit the profile set by the VC client. In many cities, conferences and events are also organized to match entrepreneurs with capital investors. For example, First Tuesday grew in 2000 to become the largest worldwide networking organization for information technology (IT) entrepreneurs and venture capitalists; its monthly events gathered 500 to 1,000 people in cities such as New York, London, and Paris. Finally, business plan and entrepreneurship competitions also allow entrepreneurs to get in front of VCs. For example, among business schools, Kellogg (Northwestern University), MIT, Baruch College, Columbia, and Cambridge (England), organize such screening events, as do some accounting firms such as PricewaterhouseCoopers. It all adds up to the fact that entrepreneurs seeking funding either should meet the VC in person or should have been personally recommended by a trusted adviser.

The first review of the written material is often done by an analyst. Partners have considerable time constraints, spreading their professional lives between fund-raising, deal making, and portfolio supervision. They like to make their own deals, developing relationships with management and following up key aspects of the business. The partner in charge will often review the deal with other partners, thereby ensuring some level of backup and reality check.

Typically, the entrepreneur is expected to make a formal presentation to the partners of the VC firm. If the entrepreneur and management team pass this test, the due diligence period begins. This is a two-way process: The VC checks out the client, while the client checks out the VC. At this point, the entrepreneur might seek a confidentiality agreement (otherwise known as a nondisclosure agreement, or NDA), but most VC firms, especially the largest and most prominent, rarely sign such documents. Considering the long-term relationship that is emerging at this stage, the entrepreneur should offer all the help that the investor requests. Any misrepresentation could become a costly deal breaker.

VCs generally capture their intentions on a term sheet. This non–legally binding document is a summary, open to negotiation, of the terms that will be set forth in a final agreement. In most VC firms, an agreement of the partners is required before the term sheet can be issued. Much of the problem during the Internet bubble of the late 1990s was that VC firms relaxed their due diligence standards, often issuing term sheets before the partnership had the opportunity to review and approve them. The idea was to be first in line because of the highly competitive nature of the market. So instead of performing due diligence and then issuing a term sheet, the process was reversed. If the VCs then discovered problems with the investment, they would renege on the term sheet.

The role of the venture capitalist is to assist the new entrepreneurs to achieve their growth objectives, using whatever resources, experience, and contacts are available. Venture capitalists act as coaches to the management of portfolio companies. They may help the company to recruit strategic partners, customers, vendors, and executive talent. During the initial stage—roughly the first six months—they can spend much of their time working with the management team of a new investment. After this period, VCs work mainly at board level and review weekly or monthly financials, which might still represent around 20 percent of their time.[3] In those circumstances, a VC partner could reasonably follow up five to seven portfolio companies.

Venture capitalists are not looking for everlasting commitment; they are more concerned with how the entrepreneurs intend to recover the VC's original investment and a high enough return on capital within four to seven years. VCs are investors who provide funds for a limited term, helping to build up a business, and then cashing in on those investments by selling their positions.

The venture capitalists adopt an exit strategy to realize the promised return on their capital. This strategy is a critical factor that influences the decision of the investor to invest, and specific exit clauses can even be included in the deal agreement. There are two primary ways of making an exit: through a public offering (where the venture capitalists sell their ownership to the public) or through the sale of the company, including the venture capitalists' ownership, to someone else (usually a large company).

## THE FUNDING PROCESS

Edgy VCs sometimes complain of entrepreneurs who "don't know the process." The steps taken by the venture capitalist between receipt of a proposal and the signing of the deal are described in the following sections. There are four stages: initial meetings, due diligence, negotiations, and closing.

### Initial Meetings

As mentioned earlier, venture capitalists often give priority to deals sent by people they know, either because they have met the entrepreneur or because the referral is from someone the VC trusts.

The first review of the written material is typically done by analysts. They will review the executive summary, and if still interested they will then request and review the whole business plan. After reviewing the proposal submitted by the entrepreneur, the analyst summarizes the deal in a specialized form or internal database, and briefs the partner if the proposal shows some value for the firm. At this stage the partner might call the entrepreneur directly and ask for a few clarifications over the phone. If all goes well, the venture capitalist invites the entrepreneur and his or her management team for a more detailed interview.

When the investor and the entrepreneur meet for the first time, there is inevitably a certain amount of nervousness in the air. For the entrepreneur, the meeting is very much like a job interview, and making a good first impression is critical. The entrepreneur will present an outline clearly describing growth prospects and profitability forecasts along with the usual display of enthusiasm.

Many entrepreneurs think they need to show slides or display jumbo-sized flip charts at the meeting. In fact, this is unnecessary: Most venture capitalists are not interested in watching a long professional presentation. The entrepreneur is better off bringing a model or a few product samples, or perhaps a picture book that clearly describes the operating units and illustrates how new technology operates within the company. The presentation should be short and focused on selling the company. VCs are fast learners, and they have already reviewed the business plan or at least its summary. Again, the goal is to sell to a sophisticated buyer. Therefore, the entrepreneur can go straight to the important points: market size, growth rate, products or services to be sold, and "why we will win." The presentation should be smooth, enthusiastic, and never boring. Forty-five minutes to an hour is probably a good target.

The venture capitalist will often also want to pay a visit to the entrepreneur and his or her company, even if it is a start-up with few visible assets. During all these meetings, the venture capitalist will not only be looking at the various items spelled out in the entrepreneur's business plan or presentation, but will also be assessing the character of the entrepreneur himself. Every venture capitalist is looking for different characteristics in each entrepreneur depending on the venture capitalist's field of specialization and the entrepreneur's area of business.

Almost every investor wants to see a positive attitude and evidence of good character traits on the part of the entrepreneur, without which the VC almost never invests. This covers integrity, loyalty, honesty, enthusiasm, creativity, leadership, a sufficiently wide knowledge base, and the physical and mental energy to complete the tasks within the allotted time frame. It is thus imperative that the entrepreneur understands his own potential, or what makes him stand out from others. For example, if the entrepreneur is weak in creativity, he may bring one of his most creative team members with him to respond to questions from the investor. It is very much a team effort.

**Due Diligence**

Before an agreement is made between the two parties about the terms and conditions of the investment, the investor will conduct due diligence on the investee company. This means carrying out background checks on the company's management team, cross-checking facts and data about the industry, and checking representations in the entrepreneur's investment proposal. The venture capitalist will try to root out misrepresentations that may be present in the entrepreneur's proposal, or any other anomalies that might give the VC reason to doubt the soundness of the investment.

As a first step, the venture capitalist interviews management, if it was not done at an earlier stage, and visits the company's premises. The starting point in any such visit is normally a Cook's tour—a tour of the entire operation, with introductions along the way to key people in the company. During such a tour, the venture capitalist tries to see as much of the business and as many people as possible. The VC may stop along the way and ask questions of the employees, trying to understand the type of people needed to make the business successful, and will absorb as much visual information about the business as possible. This is a formidable task: to learn enough about the entrepreneur's business in 30 to 60 days to invest in it with confidence.[4]

During the tour, the entrepreneur clarifies various aspects related to the company's operations, introduces the venture capitalist to key operations people, and explains the role of each. Next, the entrepreneur explains the bottom line of the business, to help the venture capitalist better understand the functions—such as purchasing, accounting, and manufacturing—that are required to deliver the end product or service to the customer.

Sometimes, however, it is not possible to conduct a Cook's tour—in the case of a start-up company, for instance. A start-up company often has no existing operation, although it may well already have leased office space for the company's operational team. Some venture capitalists will nonetheless make a trip to see these initial preparations in order to observe the management team on its own turf, and to help them better understand the cooperation among members of the team.

After the Cook's tour, the venture capitalist will want to know more about the industry, the products, and other important issues. The venture capitalist will ask for the details of every key aspect of the business. The entrepreneur needs to answer questions without hesitation to create the impression that he is on top of everything. Hesitating or not knowing something will result in the question being posed anew to the entrepreneur along with a request for his earliest possible response.

The venture capitalist may also need to sit down with industry experts. An idea may seem unique to the venture capitalist, but it will be old hat to people with more insight in the industry. It does not take long for a venture capitalist to determine whether the entrepreneur has a unique approach to a problem or if it is just a variation on a theme.

The venture capitalist will tend to ask personal questions in order to get a feel for the kinds of personalities that exist within the entrepreneur's management group. The venture capitalist wants to know how strong the entrepreneur is in handling the expected pressures of the business. Has the entrepreneur understood the time and energy he or she will need to run the business? Is the family aware of this and prepared to support the entrepreneur? What are the entrepreneur's motivations? In other words, what does success mean to him? What makes him tick?

The venture capitalist may spend many hours conducting due diligence prior to making an investment decision. There are four activities usually associated with this activity: management assessment, market assessment, product/service assessment, and financial analysis. The greatest time allocation is usually given to management assessment.[5] The venture capitalist will hold meetings with staff to learn more about the industry, the competitive marketplace, production, inventory control, labor, and cash flows. The VC may work with a marketing research firm to conduct a study of the industry and its products. He may hire production consultants to verify the manufacturing arrangements. Also, he may call upon the entrepreneur's suppliers to find out how much they are paid, what they like about the company, and the nature of their relationship with the entrepreneur. Customers, or prospective customers in the case of early-stage ventures, will be contacted. Management references will also be sought.

While the venture capital firm is conducting its due diligence, the entrepreneur must conduct his or her own due diligence on the venture capital company. The entrepreneur should know whether the venture capitalist has enough money to invest in further financing rounds. Contact ventures in the VC firm's portfolio. Learn how the VCs do business, how well they support their companies, and how they react when things don't go so well. The entrepreneur also needs to know whether the venture capitalist can bring outside expertise and open doors—for example, customers, executive talent, other investors, and foreign contacts. Those are the intangibles that make venture capital smart money.

## Negotiations

If the results of the due diligence process are satisfactory, the venture capitalist may then decide to move to the next stage: negotiation. In all likelihood, the main negotiation point is the valuation of the venture, which will decide the number of shares that the investor firm will receive in exchange for its participation. If the entrepreneur is raising $500,000 in a first round, and the premoney valuation is $1.5 million, the VC will receive a 25 percent stake of the postmoney equity. *Premoney* means that the valuation is considered before the round of financing. The term *postmoney* refers to the sum of the premoney plus the money invested in that round.

During this stage, the venture capitalist will generally have the upper hand, unless the entrepreneur has managed to attract several investors. However, it is accepted that this kind of negotiation must produce a win-win solution. To this end, attorneys have created sets of boilerplate clauses that are generally accepted as being fair to both parties.

If the VC rejects the business plan, the entrepreneur can offer to make changes and submit a better plan. If the venture capitalist is intrigued by the technology or potential market, or sees a gap in the logic shown in the entrepreneur's business model and that gap is later closed, the VC might consider investing at a later date. The entrepreneur should not interpret this as an open invitation to keep presenting to the venture capitalist in the hope that eventually he or she will cave in and invest. Although VCs are known for never saying a straight "No," if they do not specify the circumstances under which they might change their minds, then the dialogue should be considered closed for the time being.

As we noted earlier in this chapter, the VC will summarize his terms in a term sheet, sometimes called a letter of intent (LOI), that is non–legally binding and helps clarify the terms in written form. The term sheet is an important document, as it captures explicitly and implicitly a great deal of the future relationship between the entrepreneur and the VC. The entrepreneur should review it with legal counsel, and perhaps also with mentors or advisers familiar with the process.

## The Closing

After due diligence has been completed, the lawyer for the venture capitalist will contact the entrepreneur's counsel to complete the requisite legal documents for the funds transfer. These documents will be followed up with a letter of commitment stating that the investor's lawyers will send the copy to the entrepreneur and his lawyers.

Each document necessary for the closing has specific objectives and covers separate ground. If all the requisite documents are not present at closing, the parties will not be able to close the deal. In large deals the lawyers may get together the day before the closing date to see if all the papers are in order. This is called "dry closing," because no money changes hands. Simply picking a date and showing up for a closing is practically certain to result in the closing being aborted.[6]

## THE MOTIVATION OF VENTURE CAPITALISTS

Venture capital firms realize that they make money by identifying promising innovations early, investing capital to build the venture, and aiding the entrepreneur to grow his or her business. What, then, do they get in return? This section will explain the two primary motives for investing in entrepreneur firms: first, the promise of high return on investment, and second, self-actualization and accomplishment.

### High Return on Investment

In general, the capital invested by VC firms originates in less-specialized institutions, such as pension funds. Such institutions invest in venture capital funds because of the historically superior returns such funds have earned relative to other investments. Over long periods, venture capital is the highest-returning asset class available to large institutions. Of course, it is also the riskiest.

To continue attracting capital, venture capitalists must achieve returns in line with investor expectations. Because many projects will ultimately fail or provide disappointing results, only projects with high growth potential are considered. When evaluating proposed investments, a venture capital firm will weigh up the various risks, the length of time its money is likely to be tied up, and the level of returns it needs to deliver to its investors. Even if most of the firms in its portfolio disappoint, the venture capital firm may still enjoy excellent total returns. The key is finding one or two stars.

## Self-Actualization

In the early years of the venture capital industry, some of the motivation for investing came from the satisfaction of helping to build successful businesses. These early venture capitalists were fascinated by the very idea of investing, and were particularly drawn to the idea of applying innovative technologies and encouraging entrepreneurship. Many just loved the thrill of the deal. For such investors, the venturing business was a form of entertainment. They found it great fun and hugely satisfying to work with entrepreneurs and their companies and watch new technologies develop. Simply put, the venturing businesses accomplished their self-actualization needs.[7]

Venture capitalists sat on boards as partners of the entrepreneurs, played a role in corporate governance, and were involved in most major decisions. These early VCs worked for real companies that produced real things. This played into their desire to help entrepreneurial firms beyond simply giving them money. Venture capital was not just a financial transaction. VCs saw themselves as builders of companies rather than mere investors. They were in the business of creating businesses, and sometimes creating industries.[8] Today, there are still plenty of opportunities for experienced, motivated people to help entrepreneurs create wealth.

## GOING INTO BATTLE: HOW TO WIN OVER VENTURE CAPITALISTS

Compared to angel investors, the criteria imposed by venture capitalists are decidedly more complex. For the VC, funding investee companies is not a hobby, and a venture capitalist is not acting in an individual capacity but rather on behalf of a firm. Another key difference is that VC firms have fiduciary responsibilities to their investors; the same cannot be said for angels because they invest on their own behalf.

The venture capital business is a humbling one, in the sense that humbling events occur on a daily basis. This is because of the highly competitive and intense nature of a business where failures occur continuously. These might not be investment failures; they might be failures in terms of the people hired and the business relationships maintained. For this reason, the venture capitalist must be able to assess each event, learn from it, and rebound from it. As a tool for selecting which project to finance, and to minimize the risk of failure, the VC determines the criteria for entrepreneurs seeking to submit proposals requesting funding.

In this light, any entrepreneur approaching a venture capitalist should consider a range of both external and internal factors.

External factors include choosing the type of venture capital fund that best fits the entrepreneur's situation, getting a referral, and conducting a risk assessment and market competitive analysis. Internal factors include the existence of both a sound management team and a clearly articulated business plan. We now look at each of these points in turn.

**Choose the Right One**

Before approaching venture capitalists, the entrepreneur needs to short-list VC firms with investment profiles that are aligned with their needs, in order to get a feel for whether the entrepreneur's line of business matches the investment parameters and skills of the venture capitalist. The selection process may be looked at from many angles, from geographical location to industry specialization.

Seen in geographical terms, venture capital firms prefer to invest in companies that are close to their own locations. The main reason is that it is easier for the venture capitalist to meet the company's management. Another reason is that VC firms tend to locate their offices in areas that are particularly fertile in terms of the number of good companies to invest in, and thus do not need to look outside their own neighborhoods. Entrepreneurs, by the same token, are usually more attracted to areas with an infrastructure of venture capital firms and professional service providers working with start-up or emerging companies. This has obvious time- and cost-saving benefits.

If an entrepreneur is unable to raise the capital from a local venture capital group, it may be that the local venture capitalists do not wish to invest in that industry. The entrepreneur may have to look in another area for a specialist in the same field of business. In this case, the entrepreneur should explain that he has traveled a long way to find a specialist and a partner, rather than just to find capital.[9]

The entrepreneur should try to identify venture capital firms specializing in his or her field. This is invaluable to the financing process, where by far the largest amount of time will be devoted to the investigation of the industry in which the start-up firm operates. Later, it will also facilitate the provision of assistance by the venture capitalist in developing the entrepreneur's business into a successful one.

After entrepreneurs have identified a number of candidate venture capital firms, they should check the background of these firms further. After all, once entrepreneurs have obtained money from a venture fund, they will have to live with that venture capitalist for a very long time. The more the entrepreneurs know about the choice of VCs before settling on the most suitable, the better. Information about venture capital companies is now widely available on the Web, as most venture capital firms have web sites.[10] Entrepreneurs need to learn and understand what a prospective venture capitalist is really looking for prior to submitting a proposal.

### Get a Referral

A referral from an important and respected party will help draw attention to the entrepreneur. Otherwise his will be one out of several hundred applications that come in unsolicited. The existing relationship between the referral source and the venture capitalist gives assurance that he or she would send only quality deals to the venture capitalist, and that the entrepreneur's company qualifies as such. Suitable referral sources include firms in the support service sector (such as attorneys, accountants, consultants, and insurance agents), business associates, and intermediaries (such as advisory groups and placement agents). The rationale of these referral sources is that the entrepreneur who is successful in securing funding from the venture capitalist may become a major client and a lucrative source of future business. The entrepreneur may be charged for the time spent making introductions on the entrepreneur's behalf or, alternatively, be asked for a referral fee.

Other venture capitalists can also be valuable referral sources for the entrepreneur. Venture capitalist networks help the entrepreneur gain access to other VCs whose capacities and competencies are more in tune with the business. The venture capitalist may also need to draw on these networks especially when trying to secure the next round of capital, when the total amount of funds required is usually greater and the corresponding risk can be spread around.

An entrepreneur is well advised to attend venture capital conferences and meet investors. If the entrepreneur has mutual friends or knows people of similar background, such contacts will enhance his or her credibility. However, even the entrepreneur who cannot secure a referral from anyone can still attract venture capital by relying on the company's internal strengths, such as knowing what the venture capitalist is looking for and coming up with an excellent business plan.

## Conduct a Risk Assessment and Market Competitive Analysis

The entrepreneur must prove to the venture capitalist that he or she has taken into account all the major risks associated with the business. A keen and realistic understanding of the venture's risks will facilitate the fund-raising process and impress potential investors.

The secret to showing one's risk management ability is to adopt a specialization approach. Any products or services on offer should fit into a global niche. The entrepreneur must ensure that the company not only addresses a need, but that the need is a compelling one. Research conducted into prospective customers' attitudes toward existing products will help. The venture capitalist will also want evidence of the entrepreneur's ability to attract customers.

Venture capitalists will not finance a business if they perceive that the market associated with that business is too narrow, demand too limited, or profit margins too small. Likewise, if the entrepreneur's target market is mature, with several established competitors, venture capitalists will likely conclude that the opportunity is either too limited or too late.

## Have a Sound Management Team

Generally speaking, most venture capital firms focus more on the capabilities of the entrepreneur's management team than on any other factor. It has become something of a cliché in the VC business that VC firms invest in people rather than physical assets.

Some venture capitalists advise entrepreneurs to form an experienced team that has the relevant skills for the company's business field before contacting potential investors. VC firms are willing to contribute the expertise of their partners as well as capital, but they will not back companies with glaring weaknesses in management.

Venture capitalists want to see passion and commitment in the entrepreneur's management team, both toward the company and toward the execution of the business plan. They will not support an entrepreneur who is enamored of an idea or a plan whose flaws he cannot grasp and whose risks he cannot understand. Many entrepreneurial teams fail to impress during their initial meeting with potential capital providers because they appear either excessively or insufficiently passionate about the business opportunity.

The venture capitalist prefers to invest in people with high energy levels, a commitment to achievement, leadership skills, self-confidence, and a creative approach to problem solving. Flexibility and the willingness to accept counsel are also valued attributes. All aspects of an entrepreneur's personal life can provide decision-making fodder for the venture capitalist, and may be explored during the interview. The entrepreneur must be prepared to answer personal questions and should not get defensive or be surprised when the range of questions is both broad and deep.

**Prepare a Clear Business Plan**

The venture capitalist will not buy into a company that does not have a strong and effective business proposal on the table. A venture capital firm might see between 100 and 500 proposals a month. Of that number, perhaps 10 to 20 will be of some interest. Of those, three to five will receive a fair amount of analysis, investigation, and negotiation. And of those three to five, one or two may be funded. This funneling process of selecting one out of a hundred or more takes a great deal of time. It should be no surprise, therefore, that the venture capitalist sets great store in a well-prepared business proposal as an initial yardstick for measuring the capability and intelligence of the entrepreneur.

The most important quality of any business plan is succinctness built around a compelling story. A business plan should describe clearly what kind of business and industry the company is in. It will usually include an executive summary covering the high-potential market opportunity, the company's unique capabilities to serve the market, and the nature of any competitive advantage. The executive summary is expanded in the company review, which gives a more detailed explanation of the company's business objectives, company history, company mission and business model (opportunity), product uniqueness, industry and market analysis, customer profile and marketing plan, operations, facilities, and suppliers. The company review will also contain a detailed description of the company's management team, describing major accomplishments and strengths, the team's organizational structure, and key individuals. The entrepreneur will also be expected to provide a financial history (where applicable) and projections, including income statements, balance sheets, and cash flows, and, of course, the amount of funding sought.

Some entrepreneurs try to make their proposals as impressive as possible. But in the venture capital business it is an accepted axiom that no deal is perfect; every deal has something wrong with it. What the entrepreneur needs to do is to keep the proposal as error-free as possible, and convince potential investors that a certain problem is not critical and will not seriously impact the business. The entrepreneur should then conduct research to obtain additional information that will remove the item from the venture firm's perceived critical list.

## MORE ABOUT THE KEY PLAYERS

Venture capitalists tend to have well-recognized reputations and a more professional approach than angel investors. They come from a wide variety of backgrounds and exhibit a broad range of characteristics. As with angels, venture capitalists come in various shapes and sizes, each with their own characteristics. Before the entrepreneur puts forward a business plan to the venture capitalist, he or she must select the right type of venture capitalist to whom to submit the proposal. This means finding a potential investor whose investment profile best fits the company's needs.

The technical complexities of structuring venture capital are better left to legal experts than to general managers. But the subject of corporate structure within a venture capital firm is critically important to understand. The firm's structural features, like profit-sharing rules and contract terms, will certainly affect the decisions of everyone involved—entrepreneurs, intermediaries, and fund providers.

The importance of contract terms can be seen in the limited partnership structure that imposes a healthy discipline of self-liquidating the funds after a fixed period of time. For one thing, it forces investors to take the necessary but painful step of "pulling the plug" on underperforming firms in the portfolio. On the down side, however, self-liquidating can also damage the long-run prospects of entrepreneurial firms. This is known as "grandstanding." Grandstanding is the result of rushing young firms' IPOs through in order to demonstrate a successful track record—even if the investees are not ready to go public.

There are essentially four kinds of structures that may be

adopted by the venture capitalist: publicly traded, closed-end funds; public venture capital; (private) limited partnerships; and corporate arms of big companies.

## Publicly Traded Funds

Publicly traded funds, with a closed-end format, are the quintessential modern type of venture capital, first raised by American Research and Development (ARD).[11] The closed-end fund structure offers some liquidity in order to attract a broader spectrum of investors, including those with small amounts to invest. Before, opportunities in the sector were limited mainly to a few elite investors with millions or even tens of millions of dollars to invest. The liquidity has been achieved because shares in the fund can be freely bought or sold by anyone on a public stock exchange. Instead of the venture capitalist having to repay funds to investors who have lost interest, investors can sell their shares to other investors. This provision allows the fund—managed by venture capitalists—to invest in illiquid private firms, secure in the knowledge that it would not need to return its capital to individual investors. Thus, the investment horizon differences are bridged because the capital can be retained longer to match the long-term horizon of these start-up firms.

However, this kind of corporate structure has important drawbacks that limit its attraction as a device for raising VC finance. One problem is the inappropriate sale of funds by stockbrokers to unsophisticated investors, especially the elderly, who may need high current income rather than long-term capital gains. As a result, managers of such funds sometimes find themselves harassed by their investors, although it is really the brokers who are to blame for wrongly communicating the investment horizon to individuals.

Being a public company always involves a certain degree of hassle and pressure. The company must comply with SEC rules (or whatever rules, usually similar, that might prevail in their own country), and is under constant scrutiny by a large number of analysts watching to see if the company meets expectations. This makes the fund manager's job a difficult one. If a VC fund manager can raise finance from pension funds, corporations, and insurance companies, why bother with the hassles of public exposure? This attitude has caused a loss of popularity among publicly traded funds in the VC business.

## Public Venture Capital

Public venture capital began in the United States with the passage of the Small Business Investment (SBI) Act of 1958. The Small Business Administration, a federal agency created to promote growth in the entrepreneurial sector of the economy, grants licenses to eligible venture capital firms. These firms can then borrow funds at attractive interest rates (thanks largely to federal government guarantees) in exchange for certain restrictions on deal structures and on the types of businesses in which they can invest.[12] Under this program, many so-called small business investment companies (SBICs) raised significant funds very quickly. All too frequently, however, unscrupulous operators were granted SBIC licenses, in some cases backing fraudulent enterprises.[13] Still, the SBIC program was, and continues to be, an integral part of the venture capital community. SBICs, together with publicly traded funds, filled a void from the late 1950s until the early 1970s, when the limited partnership structure became the norm in the venture capital business.

On the international stage, it was not until the 1990s that public venture capital programs began to proliferate. Between 1989 and 1999, venture capital activity outside of North America grew by more than 300 percent.[14] Numerous governments, attracted by the jobs and technological innovation generated by venture capital in the United States, strove to stimulate similar development in their own countries. As a result, venture funds have received direct capital investments, loan guarantees, and targeted tax breaks from their home governments. Most of these public programs are targeted expressly at young, growing companies.

## Limited Partnerships

Limited partnerships have been, and continue to be, the dominant legal and organizational structure in the venture capital business. These pools of capital can range from $50 million to several billion dollars.[15] As in publicly traded funds, investors (known here as limited partners) supply capital for venture capitalists (managers of the fund who serve as *general* partners) to invest. Limited partners can be pension funds, corporations, wealthy individuals, university endowments, large foundations, or insurance companies.

An important contributing factor to the increase in money flowing into limited partnerships in the United States was the 1979 amendment to the "prudent man" rule governing pension fund investments. The rule stated that pension fund managers had to invest their funds' resources with the care of a "prudent man"—that is, carefully and conservatively. Consequently, it was deemed too risky for pension managers to invest heavily in venture capital. The U.S. Department of Labor's clarification of the rule explicitly allowed pension managers to invest in high-risk assets. That clarification flung the door wide open for pension funds to invest in venture capital.

Limited partners are passive investors with little or no control over how funds are used by the VC firm. These investments are made in the knowledge that venture funds are for long-term investors only. Limited partners receive their investments back in the form of shares after the partnership is disbanded (typically 8 to 10 years after the initial investment, though in some circumstances the period can be extended). This method of payment, in the form of shares, allows investors to choose when to realize the capital gains associated with their investments in the fund, and thus affords important tax advantages.

The limited partnership structure allows venture funds not only to raise capital without being publicly listed on the stock exchange, but also to choose and manage investments more successfully. The general partners perform this function, find the investments, and run the partnership. They are the ones who take on the most risk, but are well compensated for their efforts. Also, they tend to be the public face of the partnership. Thus, entrepreneurs seeking funds from such partnerships—Sequoia Capital, Kleiner Perkins Caufield & Byers, and New Enterprise Associates being well-known examples—will deal with the general partners and probably never meet the limited partners.

## Corporate Venture Capital

The history of corporate venture capital starts in the mid-1960s, about two decades after the first publicly traded funds

were formed.[16] The amount of funds available for such investment is hard to measure, because any corporation can dip into
its cash reserves and finance any investment it wants to. And
what separates venture capital from other sorts of investment
is not always obvious.

Corporate venturing sometimes resembles a limited partnership, with self-contained entities, or it may comprise
loosely organized programs set up inside the company. Corporate venture capital is usually set up as a separate arm of
the company for investment in businesses that have some
strategic affinity with the parent. To put it another way, these
investment vehicles are usually designed to seek out investments that are congruent with the parent company's strategy
or that provide synergy or cost savings. This strategic affinity
is what distinguishes corporate venture capital from other
types of venture capital.

Today, many of the world's largest technology companies
have a venture capital arm. Prominent examples include Intel,
General Electric, and Siemens. Often the investments made by
corporate venture capital play a similar role to research and
development, namely, as a source of innovation and new product ideas.

Some invest in a range of companies to ensure that they
have a bet placed on the next hot technology. Others finance
their suppliers. An important distinguishing characteristic of
corporate venture capital is that it is less prone than other
forms of VC finance to playing the star strategy (i.e., looking
for one or two big stars, while tending to ignore the rest). In
other words, they take an active, ongoing interest in a larger
percentage of companies in their portfolios than, say, a typical
limited VC partnership.

## LEVERAGED BUYOUTS

In 1974, the U.S. Congress enacted the Employee Retirement Income Security Act (ERISA), a daring and farsighted piece of legislation that locked in pension plan rights for millions of Americans. The importance of this reform can hardly be overstated, because of its role in the single most important development in capital markets over the past 50 years: the veritable explosion in pension funds and other forms of institutional investment. Large pools of investment capital would come to be managed by professional fund managers who cared only for the highest returns possible on their portfolios. With management fees based on the size of investment portfolios, and with tens and eventually hundreds of billions of dollars up for grabs, the stakes for money managers were huge.

But in the years surrounding ERISA, corporate performance was subpar, especially in the United States. The average return on capital of American companies declined by 50 percent from 1966 to 1980.[17] When mediocre corporate profits are combined with an increased pressure for high investment returns, something has to give, and it did. Fund managers began looking for explanations to help them better understand why so many companies were delivering such poor performance, and found part of the answer in shoddy corporate governance practices. In short, too many companies were run for the benefit of a close group of corporate insiders, to the detriment of shareholders. This problem has been around forever, of course, and as recent events such as the collapse of Enron and WorldCom show, it never seems to go away. Still, where there is underperformance there is also opportunity.

In the early 1980s a group of entrepreneurs began to see possibilities to enhance corporate value by replacing value-destroying managers with others who were much more focused on performance. These opportunities, combined with readily available financing, particularly from Michael Milken's junk bond unit at Drexel Burnham Lambert (discussed in the next chapter), led to a wave of hostile takeovers. They also enabled a wave of leveraged buyouts (LBOs), in which a small group of insiders bought companies mainly with debt financing.

Large LBO firms began to emerge, such as Kohlberg Kravis Roberts & Company (KKR), which aimed to unlock value by taking on debt, acquiring a company, and then dismantling it or selling off assets to pay off the debt. By 1989, when the market peaked, LBOs accounted for 20 percent of all merger and acquisition activity in the United States. While LBOs in more recent years have accounted for a far smaller percentage of M&A transactions, in dollar terms the market is nearly as large today as it was in its glory days.

The term *LBO* is sometimes used synonymously with *going private* because it often (though not always) involves the transformation of a publicly traded company, or a division of one, into a privately held firm. When performed by managers of the company, the LBO may also be known as a management buyout (MBO); when bought by an outside financial group, it's a management buy-*in*.

The typical LBO involves four distinct phases. In stage one, the buyers raise the cash required for the buyout and devise an incentive system for management. About 10 percent of the total, give or take a few percentage points, will be put up by the main investor group (which consists of the managers who will run the company, as well as possibly other parties). Outside investors, such as LBO specialist firms, provide the remaining equity. The managers also receive stock options or warrants that allow them to increase their percentage ownership if certain financial targets are reached. Most of the remaining cash (usually about 50 to 60 percent of the total purchase price) is raised from secured, or collateralized, loans (hence the term *leveraged* buyout). This debt can be provided by any combination of banks, insurance companies, or limited partnerships that specialize in venture capital or LBO investments. The rest of the cash comes from junior or subordinated debt, sometimes raised by private placements with institutional investors and sometimes by the issuance of junk bonds.

In stage two, the sponsor group either buys all of the outstanding shares of the company or buys all of the assets and transfers them to a newly formed company. Some of the assets of the acquired business might be sold off immediately to pay down the debt.

In stage three, management strives to improve performance by employing methods similar to those undertaken by businesses everywhere, including better working capital management and asset utilization; tighter cost control; and broad improvements in product quality, pricing, and customer service. The difference here is that LBOs create a sense of urgency that most other businesses lack. Cash flows must be raised quickly, or the company will fail. Although it may take several years for this process to run its course, substantial efficiency gains are looked for almost immediately. Much of the public policy debate over such efforts is that early cost savings are sometimes achieved through aggressive employee layoffs.

In the final stage, the original investor group cashes out, perhaps by taking the company public again or by selling out to other private investors. In the former case, the transaction may be referred to as a "reverse LBO," in that the business reverts to the same status it had before it was taken private. The main advantage of reconverting to public ownership is that it creates liquidity for existing shareholders. It should come as no surprise that candidates for reverse LBOs are companies that have largely succeeded in transforming themselves into lean, mean competitors. A study of reverse LBOs in the 1980s showed that original investor groups enjoyed, on average, 20-fold returns.[18] What's more, these spectacular returns were achieved with a remarkably short holding period: only 2.5 years on average. Clearly, riches beckoned for managers who could deliver the goods.

But regulatory changes, and the subsequent collapse of Drexel Burnham Lambert and the junk bond market, led to a sharp fall in LBO activity. The U.S. Congress enacted legislation in 1989 that compelled savings and loans to sell massive amounts of junk bonds into the market. Around that time, bank regulators began pressuring banks to reduce their exposures to highly leveraged transactions such as LBOs.

Unsound practices among LBO practitioners in the late 1980s also played an important role in the market's collapse. Researchers have since discovered that deals done in the latter part of the 1980s were far more likely to fail than deals done in the earlier part of the decade. A study of 124 LBOs in the 1980s found that while only 2 percent of pre-1985 buyouts defaulted on their debt, 27 percent of post-1984 buyouts defaulted.[19] It appears that the prices paid in the later years were too high and the resulting capital structures too highly leveraged. Even dramatic improvements in operating performance weren't enough to generate the cash flows needed to service the companies' crushing debt loads.

Compounding these developments was a severe economic recession beginning in 1990 and extending into 1992. Transactions plummeted in 1990, falling to under 25 percent of the total dollar volume of the previous year, and falling still further in 1991. Although the LBO market started growing again in 1993, it didn't even begin to approach its earlier prominence until the late 1990s. One reason for the market's comeback is that deals came to be structured more intelligently, with higher equity investments and more realistic debt loads than before. LBO specialists, such as KKR, became keenly aware of the dangers created by high debt loads and took steps to provide sufficient financial flexibility so that companies could endure an unexpected bout of poor performance. Today, equity may comprise as much as 25 percent, or even more, of the initial capital structure, compared with only 5 or 10 percent in the late 1980s.

More realistic pricing has helped, too. In the late 1980s a typical LBO was priced at 8 to 10 times the target's EBITDA (earnings before interest, taxes, depreciation, and amortization). More recently, transactions have been priced with EDITDA multiples of between 5 and 7.

Even with safer capital structures, LBOs are still, as the name implies, highly leveraged. And where there is leverage, there is also risk. But debt offers two important advantages, which explain why investor groups still turn to it for most of their financing. First, the original firm may have been underleveraged (i.e., it had too little debt), so that the increase in debt may itself be value enhancing. In short, the debt can provide investors with valuable tax shields, thanks to the tax deductibility of interest charges. It has been well documented that much of the value added from highly leveraged transactions comes from the clever use of such tax benefits.

The second advantage of debt is that it acts as a tool to discipline management. There is an old saying in the finance world, "Debt gets you out of bed; with equity you sleep in." Debt lights a fire under manager/owners, compelling them to urgently seek any and all sources of cash flow. To put it another way, debt motivates managers to achieve whatever efficiency gains may be possible from their businesses, and to do it fast. This effect is further enhanced by large wealth-creating incentives. If they can achieve sufficient productivity improvement to pay down the debt, managers can reap tremendous rewards. As one such beneficiary explained to a co-author of this book, "Five years of devilishly hard work, in exchange for wealth beyond my wildest dreams." It is the promise of such wealth that draws so many manager/entrepreneurs to the LBO model.

## NOTES

1. David Gladstone and Laura Gladstone, *Venture Capital Handbook: An Entrepreneur's Guide to Raising Venture Capital*, Upper Saddle River, NJ: Prentice Hall, 2002, p. 6.
2. Mark Van Osnabrugge and Robert J. Robinson, *Angel Investing: Matching Start-up Funds with Start-up Companies*, San Francisco: Jossey-Bass, 2000.
3. Susan Mason of Onset Ventures, interviewed by Robert Ellis at the offices of CPlane, April 14, 1999.
4. Gladstone and Gladstone, *Venture Capital Handbook*, p. 212.
5. G. H. Smart & Company, Inc., and The Ignite Group, *What Makes a Successful Venture Capitalist: Joint Report*, Chicago: Redwood City, 1999, p. 19.

6. Gladstone and Gladstone, *Venture Capital Handbook*, p. 244.
7. Stanford Robertson of Robertson Stephens and John Doerr of Kleiner Perkins Caufield & Byers, in Udayan Gupta, ed., *Done Deals: Venture Capitalists Tell Their Stories*, Boston: Harvard Business School Press, 2000, pp. 134, 373.
8. Gupta, ed., *Done Deals*, pp. 104, 155, 169.
9. Gladstone and Gladstone, *Venture Capital Handbook*, p. 29.
10. Several online directories to hundreds of venture capital firms can be found in the National Venture Capital Association (www.nvca.com), PricewaterhouseCoopers (www.pwcmoneytree.com), and the Capital Connection (www.capital-connection.com).
11. American Research and Development (ARD) was founded by Harvard Business School professor Georges Doriot and several local business leaders in 1946. Many investors shied away from the offering, because they felt the risk was too high. To overcome this, ARD's founders structured the company as a publicly traded, closed-end fund.
12. For more complete discussion please see: Paul Keaton, "The Reality of Venture Capital," *Journal of the Association of Small Business Development Centers*, University of Wisconsin–Extension Small Business Development Center, 1990.
13. Paul A. Gompers and Josh Lerner, *The Money of Invention: How Venture Capital Creates New Wealth*, Boston: Harvard Business School Publishing, 2001, p. 90.
14. Ibid., p. 191.
15. Gladstone and Gladstone, *Venture Capital Handbook*, p. 9.

16. See G. Felda Hardymon, Mark J. De Nino, and Malcolm S. Salter, "When Corporate Venture Capital Doesn't Work," *Harvard Business Review*, May–June 1983, pp. 114–120.

17. S. David Young and Stephen F. O'Byrne, *EVA and Value-Based Management: A Practical Guide to Implementation*, New York: McGraw-Hill, 2001, p. 116.

18. C. J. Muscarella and M. R. Vetsuypens, "Efficiency and Organizational Structure: A Study of Reverse LBOs," *Journal of Finance*, December 1990, pp. 1389–1413.

19. S. Kaplan and J. Stein, "How Risky Is Debt in Highly Leveraged Transactions?" *Journal of Financial Economics*, October 1990, pp. 215–246.

# 5

# Lenders: Raising Funds from Banks and Other Financial Institutions

We saw how start-up firms tap business angels or venture capital firms for funds. But the world's capital markets are dominated by large institutions—mainly banks, mutual funds, pension funds, and insurance companies—which tend to favor established businesses, where risks and rewards can be more easily evaluated and market liquidity is assured. Financial institutions are the primary means by which most individuals, especially the great mass of people without the resources to participate in new venture finance, invest in the capital markets. These savers deposit their savings in financial institutions that, in their role as intermediaries or middlemen, channel funds to the businesses that need them. In this chapter, we explore the funding alternatives offered by such institutions. While most of the capital on offer from financial institutions is targeted for big companies, there are still plenty of options available for the small business owner.

Although we still tend to think of each type of financial institution as offering a discrete set of products and services, distinct from the others, the products sold and the risks faced by modern financial institutions are becoming increasingly similar.[1] Fifty years ago, there was a distinct set of products offered by each type of institution, with little or no overlap. For example, apart from minor exceptions, only commercial banks offered business loans.[2] Today, insurance companies, finance companies, and pension funds also invest heavily in this sector. Even Merrill Lynch has gotten into the business loan area. Insurance companies were drawn into it, not only because of its profit potential, but also because the credit risk that goes with commercial lending could be used to balance other risks in their portfolios. Meanwhile, many banks have tried to get rid of their credit risk by passing it on to other financial institutions, mainly in the form of derivatives. And while insurance companies were unique in offering insurance and risk management products in 1950, today most categories of financial institutions actively compete in this market.

All financial institutions, through their role as intermediaries between private savers and businesses, perform at least one of several vital roles.[3] First, they may act as brokers. Buying and selling financial securities can be an expensive proposition for private investors, both because of the transaction costs involved and because of the costs of gathering information needed for evaluating and monitoring investments. By offering brokerage, research, and professional portfolio management services, financial institutions—such as discount brokers (e.g., Charles Schwab); full-service brokers (e.g., Merrill Lynch); and mutual fund groups (e.g., Fidelity)—can reduce transaction and information costs and, in the process, increase the incentives for private individuals to save.

A second critical role performed by financial institutions is that of asset transformation. Here, the institutions issue financial claims that are more attractive to household savers than the primarily securities issued by corporations. In this role, they acquire the equity and debt securities issued by companies, and finance these purchases by selling claims to private individuals and others in the form of bank deposits, insurance policies, and so on.[4]

Related to the asset transformation role is another service offered by financial institutions: their ability to make available

119

relatively low-risk, diversified portfolios more cheaply than private investors could ever hope to achieve on their own. This important benefit is offered principally, though not exclusively, through mutual funds, pension funds, and trust departments of commercial banks.[5] In this way, the shares offered by, for example, a mutual fund might be more attractive to a private saver than owning shares directly in a wide range of companies. What's more, shares in a mutual fund may be easier and cheaper to sell, offering important liquidity benefits to the investor.

In our discussion of the financing alternatives offered to growing businesses by these intermediaries, we begin by examining bank loans. We then look at alternative forms of debt finance, including government loans, commercial paper, bonds, leasing, and factoring. The final section explores the opportunities for equity finance, with emphasis on initial public offerings. We also examine private placements and direct public offerings.

## BANK LOANS

The profound changes that have occurred in the financial services industry over the past half century are nowhere more evident than in banking. Given that banks are typically the first financial institution growing businesses turn to for capital, we now consider the structural changes that have occurred in the banking sector, and what all this means for entrepreneurs who seek debt finance. Any business owner seeking to access the capital available from the global banking system should have at least a basic understanding of these changes and how they have shaped today's financial services industry.

The most important reality for traditional banking over the last generation has been its decline in both size and profitability. At the core of traditional banking's problems have been declines in its cost advantages in acquiring funds (the liability side of the business), while at the same time losing some of its income advantages (the asset side). The result has been an effort by banks to leave, or at least curtail, the traditional business of deposit taking and conventional lending, while engaging in a range of new and potentially more profitable activities. One problem with these activities, however, is that they are often riskier than more traditional banking functions, as evidenced by the large number of banks that have failed in recent years or that had to be taken over by more profitable rivals.

One important contributing factor to the declining profits of traditional banking in the United States was the effect of rules that prohibited banks from paying interest on checking accounts. These rules worked to the advantage of banks, at least until the 1960s, because their major source of funds was checkable deposits. Given that the cost of these funds was zero, banks had a very low cost of capital. Although savings accounts did pay interest, the rate was capped at little more than 5 percent. But the good times for bankers didn't last.

Rising inflation in the late 1960s and early 1970s led savvy investors to seek more attractive alternatives. By the late 1970s, money market mutual funds began to appear. These funds offered checking accounts but were structured in a way that allowed them to circumvent the restrictions on paying interest. As a result, millions of people took their money out of banks and put it into these higher-yielding investments. Today, checkable deposits account for less than 20 percent of bank liabilities; as recently as the 1960s, such deposits accounted for more than 60 percent of the total. The regulatory structure of the banking industry gradually caught up with these realities with a series of rules changes, starting in 1980, overturning the interest-rate ceilings. But by then the damage to the competitiveness of banks had already been done.

Just as banks were suffering on the cost side, they lost their advantages on the income side, too. Traditionally, businesses relied mainly on bank loans for new debt capital, offering bankers an effective monopoly on the provision of debt finance, apart from the largest, most creditworthy firms that could access the bond markets. But within the past 25 years, the banking industry has been badly hit by a seemingly nonending stream of financial innovations, including junk bonds, securitization, and the market for commercial paper. Perhaps the most important effect of this development is that traditional commercial banking lost the advantage it once enjoyed in the commercial lending business (and the higher returns that came with that advantage), while businesses of all sizes now have more avenues available to them for raising debt capital.

These changes have not been limited to the United States. Similar effects have been observed in Canada, in Europe, and in some Asian countries. The impact of these changes on the banking industry is much as one would expect: A growing number of bank failures and extensive consolidation of the sector through mergers and acquisitions. But bankers have responded in other ways, too. For example, some have tried to maintain their commercial lending businesses by expanding into new and riskier areas of lending such as commercial real estate and leveraged buyouts. Another response has been to fo-

cus on off-balance-sheet services and various forms of financial innovation, including those mentioned earlier, that offer
the prospect of higher margins than are found in traditional
banking. As a result of these changes, banks today bear only a
superficial resemblance to banks of the 1960s.

Off-balance-sheet activities involve the trading of financial
instruments and the generation of income from fees and loan
sales, activities that affect profits but do not appear on bank
balance sheets. As the term *loan sale* implies, the bank sells all
or part of the cash stream from a specific loan, thereby remov-
ing the loan from the balance sheet. The profit comes from
selling the loans for amounts slightly greater than those of the
original loans. But the interest rates on these loans are still
high enough to be attractive for investors, mainly large institutions such as pension and mutual funds. Fee income is generated by providing banker's acceptances (in which the bank
promises to make debt payments if the party issuing the security cannot), making foreign exchange trades on behalf of customers, and a range of other activities.

Financial innovation has been the catalyst behind many of
the changes observed since the 1970s in the financial services
industry. Some of these innovations have become so integral
to the industry, it is hard to imagine a modern financial sector
without them. Innovations take on many forms, but they have
always been driven by the never-ending desire of banks and
other major players in the capital markets to improve their
competitive positions. Changes in the economic environment,
combined with regulatory changes and advances in information technology, have helped to create these opportunities.
Automatic teller machines and home banking via the Internet
are just two examples among many. So, too, are the futures,

swaps, and options contracts that allow corporate clients to better manage currency, price, and interest-rate risks. To banks, one of the key attractions is that these risk-management tools have become important sources of fee income and commissions, as well as allowing banks to manage their own business risks.

Another important innovation has been the development of "securitization," in which a wide range of assets—such as mortgages, credit card loans, accounts receivable, automobile loans, and computer leases—are converted into marketable securities. The process works like this: A bank combines loans in pools with similar features, and sells certificates that are secured by the interest and principal payments on the original assets. This arrangement offers several advantages to bankers. First, the activity is profitable, with banks collecting fees from the securitization process. In addition, as long as the bank sells the certificates without recourse (which means that they have no liability on loans in the pool that go bad), they are not required to allocate loan-loss reserves.

A further advantage of securitization is that it frees up funds for further loans (and more profits). Just about any type of loan can be securitized as long as the candidates for the loan pool are similar regarding size, collateral, pricing, and maturity. Also, they must show reasonably predictable losses over time. Commercial loans are one type of loan that normally do not fit these criteria, because they tend to be negotiated on a contract-by-contract basis and exhibit substantially different characteristics. For this reason, commercial loans are not good candidates for securitization. More specialized lending, such as car loans and credit card receivables, are more standardized than commercial loans and have been successfully securitized.

Nevertheless, growing businesses do benefit from securitization because of its effect on capital requirements.

Capital requirements exist to protect deposit insurance funds in case a bank fails. If a bank should fail, regulators, such as the Federal Deposit Insurance Corporation (FDIC) in the United States, can either pay off depositors or arrange for another financial institution to buy the failed bank. Minimum capital requirements provide a cushion that can lower the cost of either alternative. But these requirements constrain growth and thus limit the ability of banks to take on risks that might lead to failure. One effect of off-balance-sheet lending is that because the loans disappear from the balance sheet, the capital that would otherwise be required for regulatory purposes is freed for other uses, including additional loans. This is the major benefit of securitization to growing businesses that seek debt capital from banks.

### Seeking a Bank Loan

Most entrepreneurs have experience with personal loans, and may believe, naively, that the process is similar to that of commercial loans. Personal loans—for cars, home mortgages, and so on—tend to be handled on a routine basis using personal details such as age and income. Either the loan request meets certain criteria or it doesn't. Commercial loans, in contrast, are far more varied and complex than personal loans, and thus call for a very different kind of review process.

Few business owners understand the true nature of lending, and why bankers must be so careful in where they put their funds. Consider the following example. A bank, which relies on depositors as its primary source of funds, provides a one-year loan to an entrepreneur at a net interest margin (the difference between the interest rate on the loan and the cost of funds for the bank) of 4 percent. The entrepreneur then defaults, and the entire principal is lost. To recover the lost principal, the bank must now earn the full 4 percent margin on 25 new loans of similar maturity and size. In other words, for every $1,000 it loses the bank needs $25,000 ($1,000/.04) of good loans just to break even. And this assumes a margin of 4 percent, which is higher than what many banks can realistically expect. At lower margins, the need for good loans to cover the bad ones is even more acute. This shows why bankers are reluctant to invest in high-risk ventures, a designation that pertains to most start-up and high-growth companies, and why they like collateral. Still, bank loans are available for such businesses.

In making their lending decisions, bankers often rely on checklists. One popular example is known as the 4 Cs:

Character of the borrower (reputation and honesty).

Capacity to repay (based on know-how and experience).

Conditions (such as industry economics, products, technologies, etc.).

Collateral (access to assets that can be sold off in the event of a default).

Many banks use more complex checklists, and for larger loans, credit scoring models. A typical model converts a set of financial indicators, such as key financial statement ratios, into a score that measures the likelihood of a customer defaulting on the loan. Potential customers who score above a specified level are considered good risks.

When a bank does take a gamble and the start-up venture succeeds, the payoff for the bank, in the form of interest on future loans and fees for a variety of services, can be huge. And there is plenty of anecdotal evidence to show that successful entrepreneurs tend to be loyal to the bankers who stuck by them when they were starting out.

Although practices differ from bank to bank, and from country to country, most professionals in the sector are in broad agreement as to what an entrepreneur can do to improve the odds of getting a loan. Personal impressions are important. The business owner needs to impress the loan officer from the first meeting. The aim should be to project an air of confident professionalism. Dress conversatively, show up on time, present a comprehensive business plan with credible financial projections, emphasize any relevant experience and management skills, and provide whatever documentary evidence is available to support the case for financing. Some cultures, particularly in Asia, place enormous emphasis on face-to-face contacts, but they are important in Western countries, too.

The business owner should be explicit as to how large a loan is needed, how the funds will be used, why debt is the right way to finance the firm's growth, how and when the loan will be repaid, and why this particular business is a good credit risk. Bankers like clarity, and the easier it is for the banker to understand the business, the greater the chances that the lending decision will be favorable. They value sound business judgment and evidence that proper financial controls are in place. Bankers also like to do business with entrepreneurs who have a strong strategic vision for their companies and a solid grasp of industry trends.

In addition, the entrepreneur must be prepared to answer in a forthright fashion when the banker starts questioning key assumptions behind the numbers in the business plan. This means that the entrepreneur should be financially literate, which implies that he or she has at least a basic understanding of finance and can speak the language of banking. Finally, the entrepreneur must be flexible and adaptable. Rarely is the financing proposal accepted right away. The process is likely to be an iterative one, with the banker suggesting changes, usually designed to reduce risk to the banker, and the entrepreneur then coming back with a counterproposal.

One potentially contentious area for negotiation is the personal guarantee. Although loans can be backed with assets, the bank is unlikely to be able to recover the full amount due in case of a corporate bankruptcy. A personal guarantee, in which the entrepreneur promises to make up any shortfalls, may be required by a banker before funds will be lent for a start-up. Naturally, entrepreneurs are reluctant to do this, because it defeats the purpose behind having a limited liability company. But bankers will sometimes insist on it, especially for high-risk ventures. Of course, for more stable or mature businesses, bankers tend to be more lenient on this issue.

When loan requests are turned down, it is nearly always because of one or more of the following reasons: lack of credibility in the revenue and profit forecasts (often caused by insufficient documentation), insufficient experience in the business, cash flow forecasts that raise doubts about the ability to repay the loan, lack of sufficient collateral, poor communication skills on the part of the entrepreneur, key information missing from the loan proposal, and expense forecasts thought to be unrealistically low. Also, bankers tend to resent business owners who try to play one banker against another. If multiple lending sources are sought out, diplomacy and tact are required.

If a loan is granted, one area for a business owner to pay special attention to, especially in a small, growing business, is the management of customer accounts. Bankers resent borrowers who come back asking for more cash when there is evidence that the company has become sloppy in the collection of receivables. Not only is this bad business practice, but it can be taken by the banker as a sign of poor financial controls that might extend to other parts of the business.

In the subsections that follow, we explore the most common loan products available. Understanding the alternatives is an important first step to securing loans at attractive terms, in part because of the tendency for bankers to specialize. For example, some lenders specialize in revolving lines of credit, while avoiding long-term, fixed-rate real estate loans. Other banks specialize in term loans, which means that borrowers seeking lines of credit are well advised to go elsewhere. Once managers have identified their company's financing needs, they can then go about matching those needs with the lending institution best able to meet them.

Most commercial loans are designed to assist borrowers in financing working capital needs (i.e., accounts receivable and inventory), or in making plant and equipment purchases. As common sense would suggest, this type of loan tends to be short-term in nature (because the sale of inventory and the collection of receivables should provide the borrower with the cash to pay off the loan). Purchases of long-term assets require longer finance periods (because it may take years for the asset to generate sufficient cash flows), and therefore tend to be financed over longer periods.

## Short-Term Loans

Short-term loans often take the form of lines of credit, also known as "loan commitments," in which the bank and the borrower agree in advance that the latter can draw against the credit line as needed up to some maximum limit. Within this limit, the borrower decides on the timing and the amount of the borrowings. In this way, lines of credit function much like credit cards. The main advantage of such arrangements is their flexibility, allowing the borrower who may need temporary financing as it accumulates inventory to obtain the funds it needs to operate, while then paying off the loan after sales have occurred and cash has been collected from customers.

Bankers like these arrangements, too, because they take up less of the loan officer's time. Of course, before such financing can be extended, a detailed analysis of the borrower's creditworthiness must be completed. The loan officer evaluates the purpose of the credit line, the prospects for repayment, the maximum amount that the bank is willing to lend, compensating balance requirements (i.e., bank accounts that the borrower is required to maintain), and the interest rate charged. The line of credit can be secured (with specific assets pledged against it) or unsecured; it can be fixed-rate or floating; and the underlying note can be a demand note or fixed-term. But in nearly all cases, the line of credit is short-term, often lasting only 90 days. Although lines of credit are normally confirmed in writing, the nature of the agreement is informal, with bankers reserving the right to cancel or amend the agreement at will. In addition, letters of confirmation typically state that loans may not be available if the borrower's financial condition changes for the worse.

## Long-Term Loans

Plant and equipment purchases and other long-term investments, including acquisitions of other companies, are typically financed with term loans covering periods of one to 10 years, with terms between three and five years being the most common. Term loans are designed to finance a major cash outlay and spread the repayment of the loan, including interest, over a period of time roughly corresponding with the cash flow that will be available to service the debt. Permanent increases in working capital, such as those that may arise from entering new markets, may also be financed in this way.

Term loans are usually tailored to the needs of the borrower, so no two are exactly alike. However, these loans typically include a common set of terms and conditions. Besides the obvious elements required in any loan contract, such as the interest rate and the payment period, borrowers are subjected to a series of covenants that mandate certain actions while prohibiting others. For example, the contract may specify that the borrower agrees to continue in essentially the same business over the term of the loan, to grant the bank access to its books, and to maintain adequate insurance. Submission of financial statements on a regular basis will also be required. In addition, the borrower may be prohibited from taking on other debts without the bank's consent.

It is also common for banks to impose certain financial tests on the borrower. For example, the company will be required to maintain minimum levels of working capital and not to exceed maximum levels of indebtedness, lease obligations, and dividend payments. There may also be constraints imposed on the pay raises that are granted over the loan period to certain corporate employees. Failure to meet any of these requirements will put the borrower in "technical default." This means that even if all interest and principal payments are made on time, the company has still violated the loan contract. As a result, the borrower may be required to renegotiate the debt, with new terms that are certain to be more onerous and expensive than the original contract. For many banks, technical defaults are more common than borrowers defaulting because of their inability to make the required cash payments.

Another popular form of bank lending is the "revolving credit," which combines elements of term loans and lines of credit. These are formal agreements that require the bank to lend money provided the borrower is not in default on any of the terms and conditions in the agreement. The terms and conditions of the loan are extensive, and the bank expects a commitment fee in exchange for the service. As with lines of credit, revolving credits are used mostly for funding working capital. But there are two important differences. First, the term for revolving credits can be far longer than for informal lines of credit, with one, two, or three years being the most common. Second, revolving credits are not subject to the "cleanup" provision that is a normal requirement for unsecured lines of credit. Under a cleanup, typically invoked on an annual basis, the borrower is expected to pay off all outstanding borrowings. The cleanup is designed to demonstrate that a company's need for the bank's funds is only temporary and that it has adequate capital resources to operate the business. Secured lines of credit don't follow this practice because the collateral pledged against the loan is considered sufficient protection for the bank. Likewise, revolving credits don't require cleanup. Instead, the borrower expects to be on the bank's books for the entire term of the agreement. But just as for any line of credit, banks insist on commitment fees before agreeing to revolving credits.

## GOVERNMENT-SPONSORED LOAN PROGRAMS

The U.S. Small Business Administration and similar agencies in other countries are not financial institutions in the strict sense of the term, but most of their activities can be viewed as adjuncts or extensions of commercial lending. Indeed, the most common form of state support for small business is a loan guarantee, which allows entrepreneurs to obtain loans from commercial banks that they would not otherwise qualify for.

The SBA's Section 7(a) program is its largest, and is what most people think of when they talk about SBA loans. Under this program, the agency promises to reimburse the lender in the event of default for between 50 percent and 85 percent of the principal amount, depending on the size of the loan and the specific provisions under which the guarantee is made. In all cases, it's the lender, and not the borrower, who submits the loan package to the SBA for approval. A standard loan guarantee can require several weeks or even longer for approval, but for smaller loans ($150,000 or less) or in cases where the entrepreneur can obtain a commercial loan with a smaller guarantee, the approval process can be as short as a single day.

Under its Section 504 program, the SBA makes loans itself, instead of guaranteeing loans made by commercial banks. The funds are channeled through certified development companies (CDCs), which are community-based, nonprofit corporations. Borrowers apply directly to their local CDC. Such loans are capped at $1 million, although the ceiling is raised to $1.3 million for businesses that promote certain public policy goals. For example, businesses owned and controlled by women, military veterans, or members of select minority groups are eligible for the larger loan amount. The main advantage of this program is that the loans have long repayment periods, either 10 or 20 years, considerably longer than what an entrepreneur would be likely to obtain from a commercial bank.

All SBA loan programs have specific eligibility requirements, such as size restrictions. For example, manufacturing companies should have no fewer than 500 employees but no greater than 1,500. Construction businesses should have revenues no greater than $9.5 million. Specific size restrictions are imposed for retail, wholesale, service, and agricultural businesses, too.

In addition, the business must be profit oriented, have adequate owners' equity, and show that alternative financing sources, such as personal assets, have already been tapped. Also, the borrower has to be clear about how the funds will be used—to acquire fixed assets, inventory, real estate, renovations, and so on. The uses to which funds can be put are sometimes contingent on the specific SBA program under which the loan is made. For example, Section 504 loans are limited to fixed assets, whether buying, constructing, or renovating them. A business that seeks capital to finance working capital would have to apply under a different program.

The SBA also looks at the personal attributes of the entrepreneur. Specifically, they look for good character, relevant management expertise, sufficient funds (including the SBA loan) to operate the business on a sound financial basis, a credible business plan, collateral, and evidence that projected cash flows will be sufficient to repay the loan on time. Of course, these attributes are essentially the same as the ones bankers look for.

In addition to Section 7(a) and Section 504, the SBA also funds "microloans" that are targeted at very small businesses. The maximum that can be borrowed under this program is only $35,000. The funds are lent through community-based nonprofit groups, such as a community development company (discussed earlier), but the SBA channels funds to other organizations, too. As with Section 504 loans, applications are made directly to the lending body, not to the SBA. This group makes the lending decision and imposes the terms and conditions of the loan, if approved. One important difference between this type of loan and a Section 504 loan, besides the obvious difference in loan size, is that in the case of microloans the intermediary is required to provide technical assistance and training to the borrower.

The most common complaint from entrepreneurs seeking loan guarantees is the time and patience required to fill out the paperwork and to satisfy any other requirements imposed by government officials. Commercial banks can be bureaucratic, too, but the consensus is that they are usually less frustrating to deal with than a government agency. Another potential drawback is that terms and convenants may be imposed on the borrower that are more restrictive than those normally required by banks.

## COMMERCIAL PAPER

In the United States, commercial paper is the most common form of short-term financing for large companies. Commercial paper is a contract by which the borrower promises to pay a specified amount to a lender at some date in the future, usually one to six months. Typically, the amount of the loan is rolled over, which means that it is repaid by issuing new commercial paper. As interest rates rise, however, borrowers become more likely to pay off the debt. The rapid growth of this market in recent years, in Europe as well as in the United States, has been a major reason why conventional bank lending activities play a less important role in corporate finance than they did a generation ago.

On the borrowing side, the commercial paper market is limited almost entirely to large, high-quality, low-risk companies. As we will see later, while this market may be closed to smaller ventures, there are alternatives that serve much the same purpose. Most of the funds in the commercial paper market are provided by a variety of financial institutions, including insurance companies, bank holding companies, and private consumer lenders such as Household Finance (HFC) and General Motors Acceptance Corporation (GMAC). Sometimes large financial institutions are on the borrowing side, issuing their own commercial paper directly, often to money market mutual funds.

In fact, the growth of such funds played a critical role in the growth of this market. As they attracted ever increasing funds from investors seeking interest on their checking accounts, fund managers eagerly sought out any liquid, high-quality instruments they could get their hands on. While

Treasury bills have traditionally been the staple investment for money market funds, commercial paper has the advantage of higher yields (given that it is issued by private corporations, and not by government) without a high risk of default. It should be noted, however, that commercial paper is not risk free. Declining economic conditions in the aftermath of the September 11 attacks led to several scares, and even a few defaults.

While financial institutions can issue their own commercial paper, corporations nearly always go through investment bankers. Not only did the commercial paper market take away some of banking's most attractive loan clientele, but commercial banks in the United States were formally barred under the Glass-Steagall Act from underwriting these instruments. The only paper they could issue was their own. Since 1987, however, commercial banks can underwrite and deal in securities using a so-called Section 20 affiliate. Several dozen banks have taken advantage of this provision, so that while commercial banks still lose business on the lending side to this market, they can at least compete in underwriting the securities.

## BONDS

Bonds are tradable fixed-income securities, usually with a maturity greater than one year. In essence, bonds are alternatives to commercial lending, and for those companies that can access the bond markets, bonds offer the prospect of long-term borrowing at lower rates. Bonds give companies the opportunity to access a broader group of investors, including any person or institution with money to lend.

Bond issues are usually managed through underwriters, investment banks that buy the bonds from the issuing company and then sell them to investors, at a profit of course, using their extensive sales networks. The underwriters have a difficult balancing act to perform, because while the corporate issuers seek the lowest interest rates possible, the bonds must be attractive enough to the capital markets to draw in prospective investors. Underwriters work closely with the issuer to design bonds that satisfy the financing priorities of the latter while also satisfying the demands of the capital markets. They do this by focusing on several key features.

The most important features include price, maturity, embedded options, and covenants. Price is a function of the cash flow pattern of the bond and market interest rates. For example, if the prevailing market rate for the bond a company wishes to issue is 9 percent, but the bond provides a "coupon," or interest, payment of only 8 percent, the only way that investors will buy the bond is at a discount to its par, or maturity, value. If, in contrast, the bond pays a coupon in excess of the prevailing interest rate, the bond will sell at a premium to par. In the case of the former, a significant portion of the cash flow return to the investor occurs at the end of the bond's life, while in the case of the latter, a greater amount of cash flow is offered throughout the bond's life. Investment bankers advise clients on this issue based not just on the cash flow patterns desired by the issuer, but also those desired by potential investors. Unless the bond has properties that are desirable to the investing community, especially to large institutional investors, the underwriter will find it impossible to sell the bond at a profit while at the same time providing acceptable proceeds to the issuing company.

The maturity period is the maximum length of time the borrower has to pay off the face amount, or bond principal, in full. Maturities on corporate bonds are nearly always less than 30 years, but there are bonds with longer maturities. Note that the maturity is a maximum; corporate issuers can, and often do, buy back the bonds well before they mature. Such repurchases can be motivated by changes in market interest rates, but also by the desire to reduce financial leverage.

Sometimes bonds are bought back at preset prices, a feature known as "callability." In such cases, the bond contract contains a schedule of dates specifying the prices on those dates at which the firm can call the bonds. When the call is invoked, investors have no choice but to surrender the bonds at the stipulated price. Logically, therefore, the callability feature reduces the proceeds a corporate issuer can collect when the bond is issued. To put it another way, the rate of interest that must be paid to investors is higher than it would be without the call feature. It should be noted, however, that callability is far less popular today than it was 20 years ago. Since then, its use has been limited mainly, though not exclusively, to smaller firms and to those with lower bond ratings (i.e., relatively risky issuers).

Callability is just one example of what finance professionals call "embedded options," that is, options that are embedded in the bond contract. Another example can be seen with convertible bonds, in which the bondholder has the right, but not the obligation, to convert the bond into another security, usually shares of common stock. The terms of the conversion option (including the conversion price, the earliest date at which the option can be exercised, and the number of shares each bond is entitled to upon conversion) are indicated in the bond contract. This feature has the opposite effect of callability on the bond's interest rate. Because the conversion feature has value, allowing the bondholder to take advantage of a sharp increase in the issuer's common stock, investors are willing to accept a lower rate of interest than they would if the bond was not convertible. Although convertible bonds allow the issuer to raise debt finance at a lower rate of interest, there is no free lunch here. Corporate officers must always consider the potential dilution effects on shareholders of any conversion. Like the callability feature, conversion is more popular among small firms, although some large firms use it.

Another option feature is known as "putability," in which a put option is granted to bondholders. This option grants them the right, under certain circumstances, to sell the bond back to the firm. The attractiveness of this feature to investors is that it protects them in case the company tries to increase its financial leverage dramatically through subsequent debt issues. The usual effect of such sharp rises in debt is to raise the firm's interest rates, causing the value of its existing debt instruments to fall. Putable bonds became popular after the M&A boom in the 1980s, when leveraged buyout specialists, such as KKR, imposed heavy debt burdens on the companies they took over, causing existing bondholders to sometimes suffer large losses. The now legendary KKR takeover of RJR Nabisco, dramatically recounted in the best seller *Barbarians at the Gate*,[6] is perhaps the most famous example. Investors are willing to pay a premium for protection against such eventualities, and thus putability lowers the interest rate a company pays on the bond (and increases the proceeds from the bond issue).

As noted earlier in our discussion on bank loans, covenants are the rules that specify the rights of the lender and the restrictions on the borrower. Although the discussion here focuses on bonds, as we have seen banks often impose similar rules on their borrowers. For example, asset convenants, which specify what rights the bondholder has to the firm's assets in case of default, are broadly similar to the collateral requirements commonly found in bank loans. Secured bonds have specific assets pledged to the bondholders. For unsecured bonds, companies will often establish a pecking order, with senior bonds given priority in the event of corporate liquidation over junior or "subordinated" claims.

Another type of covenant prevents firms from issuing new debt at will. And when new debt is issued, the covenant will likely require that it have a subordinated claim to the firm's assets in event of default or bankruptcy. Dividend covenants prevent firms from siphoning off cash for the benefit of the shareholders while leaving the company unable to service its debts. Other covenants impose requirements on the borrower to maintain certain levels of key financial ratios, such as interest coverage (usually measured as the ratio of pretax operating earnings to interest expense). The enforcement of these and other convenants is often left to a trustee, appointed to perform roughly the same function as a bank loan officer monitoring commercial loans. When companies violate these convenants, they are in technical default on the loan, even if they are making all of the promised interest and principal payments. Such defaults may require costly renegotiation with bondholders, and thus companies will do whatever they can to avoid them.

The bond rating agencies—principally, Standard & Poor's (S&P), Moody's Investors Service, and Fitch—are also important players in the bond market. The most obvious effect of the ratings granted by these agencies is their impact on the interest rates that issuing companies must pay on their bonds. The higher the rating, the lower the rate. But the influence of the agencies doesn't stop there. Credit ratings have become shorthand for financial safety and quality, affecting not just the rate that companies pay on their public debt instruments, but also the rates required by investors for all financial instruments, even equity. Regulators, too, rely on ratings in deciding which securities can be held by certain types of institutional investors, such as money market funds and insurance companies. For example, in some jurisdictions insurance company portfolios are allowed to hold only "investment-grade" debt instruments, meaning that only those bonds and notes that are deemed to be highly safe are eligible for inclusion. Companies that cannot secure investment-grade ratings are effectively excluded from accessing a large portion of the bond investor market.

The recent wave of financial scandals in the United States, especially the Enron fiasco, has led to an unprecedented degree of public scrutiny of the inner workings and professional competencies of rating agencies. Following the collapse of Enron in December 2001, critics asked why the company continued to be rated investment grade until just days before it was declared bankrupt. A growing consensus has emerged that the agencies' claims of being deceived by Enron management are simply unacceptable. The markets rely on the agencies to be professional skeptics, following up and asking the tough questions of management when information is sketchy or troubling facts emerge. What perhaps should be of even greater concern to the agencies is the growing sense in the investment community that rating changes (both upgrades and downgrades) often lag an issuer's creditworthiness. In other words, ratings are changed only after it has become obvious that a given company's financial strength has improved or deteriorated. Evidence of this can be seen in significant interest rate increases or decreases for companies, independent of changes in market interest rates, without any change in bond ratings. Upgrades and downgrades should lead interest rate changes, not lag them.

In response, Moody's has cut the time it takes analysts to come to a decision once a company's credit rating is up for review. Where before it took 90 days, the aim is now 60 days. Although many investors would like to see the review process proceed even faster, a responsible credit review requires meetings with company management. Preparation on both sides (company and credit rating agency) takes at least a few weeks. S&P's response to recent criticisms includes a willingness to more quickly put companies on credit watch (a sort of warning system) when its analysts think that a rating change might be in the pipeline. And, like Moody's, S&P now aims to make rating change decisions more quickly.

What does all of this mean to corporate debt issuers? Among other things, the rating agencies are now expected to pay closer attention to corporate governance and the quality of an issuer's accounts, and to raise alarms where they find either is lacking. In other words, the quality of the financial numbers has become as important as the numbers themselves. Companies without a strong reputation for financial reporting integrity and those with weak corporate governance regimes will pay a heavy price in the form of lower ratings and higher charges on capital.

The rating agencies are also putting more emphasis these days on liquidity risk, which in this case means the ability of an issuer to access short-term cash in event of a crisis. When this ability is thought to have eroded, a sharp downgrade may follow. One prominent example involved Railtrack, the United Kingdom's railway infrastructure company. The company enjoyed a high bond rating in the years following its privatization, mainly because the agencies believed that Railtrack had the backing of the British government. When the government announced in October 2001 that it would not bail out the troubled company, Railtrack's rating instantly fell from A to CC, one of the largest one-time drops in recent memory. Overnight, Railtrack's debt went from investment-grade to junk-bond status.

## Junk Bonds

Perhaps the most interesting development in bond markets over the past generation has been the growth of junk bonds. Where previously the bond market was limited to the most creditworthy businesses, the junk bond market has opened this form of financing to medium-sized and other lower-quality borrowers.

Junk bonds are securities that are classified by Moody's or Standard & Poor's as below investment grade. More specifically, this means a rating of below Ba3 from the former or BBB– from the latter. Historically, firms with ratings of, say, BB or worse were precluded from issuing bonds and had to rely almost exclusively on bank loans for debt finance. Junk bonds have always existed, but until the 1980s nearly all were "fallen angels," which means that they were investment grade (i.e., relatively safe) when issued but later downgraded as the financial condition of the issuer deteriorated.

144

The market took off in the early 1980s when several investment banks, notably Drexel Burnham Lambert, convinced investors that junk bonds were sound investments. The idea began with a master's thesis prepared by the now legendary (and notorious) Michael Milken when he was an M.B.A. student at Wharton. In his research Milken discovered that diversified portfolios of fallen angels offered highly attractive returns, more than compensating bondholders for the added risks of investing in bonds with a relatively high likelihood of default. Milken argued that while junk bonds were risky, diversification eliminated much of that risk, leaving the high returns that come from investing in risky financial instruments. Years later, while working as Drexel's junk bond specialist, he was able to put this simple, yet powerful, idea into practice.

Milken's great innovation was in extending the junk bond market beyond fallen angels to include bonds that had junk status ("speculative grade" in official parlance) from the beginning. Suddenly, companies that could never issue commercial paper or bonds were able to sell junk bonds in the new issue market. The advantages to issuing businesses were enormous. They had access to not only larger pools of capital, but also longer-term and cheaper financing than was available from their bankers. This innovation played a pivotal role in the dramatic growth of leveraged buyouts in the 1980s.

But the market suffered a huge setback in 1989 when Milken and Drexel Burnham were charged with violating securities laws. At that time, Drexel provided much of the secondary market support for the junk bonds. Very simply, if you wanted to trade in junk bonds, you had to do business with Drexel Burnham. When Drexel filed for bankruptcy in 1990, the junk bond market collapsed, along with the prices of junk bonds. The post–Gulf War recession put a further dent in the market as many junk bonds issuers defaulted, confirming that junk bonds were indeed risky. As expected, corporate business gravitated back to commercial banks, but the junk bond market gradually clawed its way back to become a major player again in providing funds for promising but risky businesses. Still, the risky nature of junk bonds is brought home to investors whenever macroeconomic performance is weak. Although not as severe as the previous 1989–1990 downturn, the year 2002 saw a wave of junk bond defaults in the United States and in Europe. A slow economy and the bust in the technology sector were cited as the major contributing factors.[7] The market turmoil caused several companies to abandon plans to issue such bonds. One prominent example was Bertelsmann, the German media giant, which was forced to put off a planned €1 billion issue in June of that year. Interest rates had risen to uneconomic levels for telecom and media companies in the immediate aftermath of the WorldCom scandal.

But the logic of the junk bond market is compelling. Just weeks after the Bertelsmann announcement, QwestDex, the phone directories business of Qwest Communications, announced a $1 billion junk bond offering. Although technically in the troubled telecoms sector, the relatively stable nature of the directories business suggested that a successful offering was possible. The continued presence of this market is one of the reasons why some banks have increased the riskiness of their loan portfolios. Not only does this practice offer higher yield spreads (i.e., higher potential profits for banks), but it also offers a way to compete directly for some of the business that would otherwise go to the junk bond market.

Throughout most of 2001 and 2002 the market in speculative-grade bonds grew, not so much because of new bond issues, but rather because of a large number of previously investment-grade bonds that suffered through downgrades from the rating agencies. In 2002, for example, the bonds of many large European companies, including Alcatel, Fiat, Ericsson, Vivendi Universal, and The ABB Group, were downgraded to junk-bond status.

Simply put, fallen angels will always be with us. But it should never be forgotten that corporate bonds, and especially those with junk status, are inherently risky. No further proof is needed than the fact that 216 companies worldwide defaulted in 2001 on $116 billion of debt.[8] The first quarter of 2002 saw a further $34 billion in defaults.

## LEASES AND FACTORING: THE ROLE OF FINANCE COMPANIES

Finance companies have been around in various forms for more than a hundred years, but they really began to take off when automobile companies set up financing arms to help people buy cars. The idea spread to sellers of other goods as they discovered that not only did finance companies make it easier for them to sell their wares, but that the finance operation itself was profitable. Eventually, business finance companies emerged to fill financing needs not well served by banks, such as leasing. And just as producers of consumer products set up financing arms, so too did the manufacturers of business products.

As we noted earlier, the commercial paper market is generally closed to small businesses. One reason for this is that the minimum investments required to participate in this market make it difficult for the smallest of businesses to participate. Finance companies allow such companies to access this market by selling commercial paper and using the proceeds to make loans. In other words, instead of issuing commercial paper directly into the money markets, small businesses access the markets indirectly through the intermediation services of finance companies. To put it another way, finance companies borrow in large amounts but tend to lend in small amounts. This practice stands in sharp contrast to commercial banks, which tend to borrow in small amounts (from depositors) and then make large loans. Major players in the United States include Household International and AmeriCredit.

An important contributing factor to the growth of this sector came from the large loan losses suffered by many banks in the late 1980s and early 1990s. Banks were then forced to strengthen their capital positions, which led to a general tightening of terms and standards for business loans. Finance companies stepped in to fill the void. By 1999, the financial assets of these institutions had growth to $956 billion from just under $200 billion in 1980.[9]

Another important reason for the huge growth of this sector over the last generation is that it is far less regulated than commercial banks and thrift institutions (such as savings and loans in the United States or building societies in the United Kingdom). Because they are deposit-taking institutions, banks are closely regulated by government agencies. For example, banks are subject to strict lending limits, which has important implications for potential borrowers. Finance companies have far more latitude than banks in the assets they hold and in how they raise their funds. As a result, finance companies can sometimes tailor loans to better suit their customers than can banks.

Also, finance companies are often willing to lend to companies that are unable to obtain bank loans. Because of their capital restrictions, most banks require loans to be of a certain quality. Either the credit application passes or it doesn't, in which case the applicant doesn't get the loan. Finance companies tend to look at loans in terms of a risk-reward continuum, in contrast to the pass-fail system of banks. This gives finance companies greater flexibility in deciding to whom to lend. It also helps to explain why their loans are often more expensive than those offered by commercial banks. Because they sometimes lend to companies with risks beyond what a bank might consider prudent, they can charge higher interest rates.

Like banks, finance companies tend to specialize. Small and middle market players are geographically focused, while larger finance companies offer national or broad regional coverage. Still, even big players tend to specialize, either by industry or by asset collateral groups. Their industry specialization allows them to better serve the financing needs of their clients. Captive finance companies (i.e., the financing arms of manufacturers) exist to finance purchases of the products produced by their parent companies. Such sources of finance can be attractive, and relatively low-cost, when a business has specific equipment needs.

To the small business owner, conventional loans are not the major service offered by finance companies. More commonly, they use these lenders for leasing and factoring, although they will sometimes turn to other financial institutions, including commercial banks, for similar services. A lease is a contract in which the owner of an asset, the lessor, gives the right to use the asset to another party, the lessee, in return for a set of fixed payments. Factoring entails the purchase by a finance company, at a discount, of a business's accounts receivable.

## Leasing

The contract between the lessor and the lessee defines the length of time for which the lessee can use the asset, the amount and timing of payments by the lessee, the party responsible for maintenance of the asset, and whether the lessee has the right to buy the asset at the end of the lease period and, if so, at what price. Most long-term leases stipulate that at least some, if not all, of the lease payments are noncancelable. This fact illustrates the single most important economic reality of leasing, one that is sometimes ignored by managers and entrepreneurs: Leasing is a form of debt and, therefore, must be managed like debt.

Because of the flexible nature of leasing and its potential tax advantages (discussed later), the volume of leasing has grown to the point that in some countries it has become the dominant form of asset financing. In fact, any asset that can be bought can also be leased, which means that the list of assets available for lease is practically endless.

Broadly speaking, there are two types of leases—financial and operating. Financial leases (also known as "capital leases") generally extend over the life of the asset, or at least most of it, while operating leases tend to be of a shorter duration. Many managers are tempted to view leases, especially those of the operating variety, as akin to rental contracts without an obvious interest-payment component or any impact on the future debt-raising capacity of the firm. This view is badly mistaken.

Because financial leases cover most if not all of the asset's economic life, most managers and business owners appreciate that such leases are simply alternatives to bank finance. This reality is made even more obvious by the accounting treatment for financial leases, which requires that they be capitalized (i.e., the future lease payments are converted into a present value equivalent) and included on the balance sheet as both assets and debts, in much the same way as an asset purchased with a bank loan would be.

To illustrate the nature of such leases, suppose that a business needs a fleet of trucks for product shipments. The firm can borrow funds to buy the trucks, pledging the trucks as collateral against the loan. If loan payments are missed, the bank claims the trucks, sells them, and recovers at least some of the amount owed. Alternatively, the business can lease the fleet of trucks. Like the banker in the case of a failed loan, the lessor can claim the trucks if payments are missed. From an economic perspective, the two alternatives are equivalent. The only difference is a legal one; in the case of the bank loan, the business firm takes legal title to the assets; when the assets are leased, legal title rests with the lessor. But either transaction can be viewed as a mortgage, with the assets pledged as collateral against the loan.

To the savvy business owner, there can only be one advantage to leasing over owning: The lease offers a cheaper financing alternative to the bank loan. This possibility arises mainly because of corporate tax laws. To illustrate, suppose an airline wants to acquire an additional plane. The airline already owns several planes, each of which is depreciated for tax purposes in the most aggressive manner allowed under the law. The practical effect, and this is common among airlines, is that it shows a loss for tax purposes, even if it shows a profit under generally accepted accounting principles. There's no trick here; the company may be using less aggressive depreciation in the financial statements it shows to the capital markets than it uses for its tax returns. This is all perfectly legal, and may even be appropriate. But if the airline were to acquire another plane, and depreciate it like the planes acquired previously, the depreciation charges offer no benefit because the company is already showing losses for tax purposes.

Contrast this situation with that of another, more profitable, airline, which continues to show profits, even under tax law. If this firm were to acquire another plane, the net cost of the investment would be the cost of the plane itself (i.e., the price paid to Boeing or Airbus), minus the present value of future tax shields because depreciation on the plane is tax deductible. The result is that the net cost of the investment in the new plane is lower for this airline than it is for the airline that cannot fully exploit the depreciation tax shield. If our company falls in the latter category, it would seem as if we are at a severe competitive disadvantage. Leasing offers a way out of this dilemma.

The lease effectively allows the airline to sell the depreciation tax shield to another party—in this case, the lessor—that can fully exploit it. In return, the airline can finance the plane at a lower rate of interest than if it were to finance the purchase of the plane with a conventional bank loan. In short, there is only one reason why a business owner should choose a financial lease over a bank loan: It is cheaper.

The economic analysis of operating leases is more complex. This complexity arises because the period of the lease is usually much shorter than the economic life of the asset being acquired. To complicate matters further, leasing companies offer a range of other services, in addition to the financing, such as fleet maintenance and record keeping. Isolating the cost of these services and determining the cost of the financing require sophisticated finance tools, such as option pricing theory. Leasing companies understand this complexity well enough, but all too often the lessee on the other side of the contract does not, a fact cleverly exploited by the former.

There are potential advantages to leasing apart from the tax benefits, but to some extent these advantages are either illusory or short-term. For example, it is often said that leasing improves a company's cash flows because little or no cash is required up front. True, but the lower the down payment, the higher the future lease payments. What's more, while the leasing arms of equipment manufacturers are eager for new customers, the implied interest rates in the financing terms they offer are likely to be high, especially for small businesses.

Another potential advantage of leasing is that it protects against obsolescence, allowing companies to easily upgrade to better or more modern equipment. But this feature, too, comes at a price. The obsolescence risk tends to be priced in the lease, making lease payments higher. Also, because the property will be returned at the end of the lease period, and the lessor (the legal owner in this case) naturally wants the asset returned in suitable condition, restrictions on how and where the equipment may be used are sometimes imposed. For example, leased vehicles may have mileage restrictions. Leased buildings may also be subjected to restrictions on improvements, thus limiting the company's flexibility in the way that it manages its facilities. In short, leasing is no free lunch.

## Factoring

Factoring is a specialized form of lending in which a financial institution, such as a finance company, buys the accounts receivable of a business at a discount to face value. The difference between the proceeds given to the business and the amount collected by the finance company from the customers of the business represents the finance company's return, or interest. Factoring is really just a type of short-term loan in which the loan is backed by specific assets (in this case, receivables).

This form of financing is particularly attractive for companies that otherwise lack the financial record required for bank loans, including start-ups. Even successful high-growth companies can benefit from factoring. The rapid expansion of inventories and receivables common to such businesses often leads to negative operating cash flows, making the company a poor candidate for conventional bank loans. Seasonal businesses, such as retailers and clothing manufacturers, are also natural candidates for factoring.

The most obvious advantage of factoring is that it is the only financing source that is guaranteed to grow with sales. As sales increase, so too do the opportunities for raising capital through the sale of receivables. Another potential advantage is that bad debt risk can be eliminated, assuming that the receivables are sold to the finance company "without recourse." This means that the seller is not obligated to compensate the finance company for uncollectible accounts. Also, because factoring provides a quick source of cash, a business can more quickly pay off its own debts, such as accounts payable, helping the company to establish a good reputation with suppliers. This benefit is especially important to a young business that actively seeks to establish a good credit history. A further advantage is that finance companies and other factoring agents can handle collections more professionally than sellers can internally. To some extent, factoring can be viewed as a way of outsourcing the collection of receivables.

But all of these benefits come at a cost, the most important being the implied interest charge. The factoring agent's profit (the difference between the amount raised from collecting the accounts receivable and the amount paid to the company) varies widely, but the interest charges are usually higher than those of comparable bank loans. This is hardly surprising given that businesses often turn to factoring because of their inability to obtain bank loans. Generally, the standard of financial strength required to obtain funds through factoring is lower. Reasonable financial statements and creditworthy customers will usually suffice. However, users of factoring should know that the process can be intrusive, a logical consequence of factoring companies having to verify and monitor the collection of customer accounts.

## EQUITY FINANCE

As we showed in Chapter 2, sources of capital are related to the growth cycle. As firms progress from start-ups to successful growth companies, and then to maturity and decline, funding sources change. The evidence on privately held firms is mainly anecdotal; in the United States, as in most countries, only public companies are required to report on such matters. But what experience does seem to show is that small, private businesses rely mainly on bank debt, leasing, contributed capital from their owners (including angels and venture capitalists), and internally generated cash flows. Firms in the earliest stages of development rely mainly on the first three sources. As firms become more established, internal cash flows come to play a more important role. Because internally generated cash flows come from profits, and profits belong to shareholders, these cash flows represent a form of equity investment. But external sources of equity finance, such as initial public offerings, generate far more interest.

Those private businesses that receive capital from angels, venture capitalists, and other private equity investors usually plan to go public eventually, partly because an IPO can serve as an effective exit strategy for these investors. However, the process of going from VC financing to an IPO is a lengthy one, requiring not only further development of the business, but also careful planning with financial advisers and navigating a complex registration process with the regulatory authorities (such as the SEC). On average, companies go public around three to four years after the injection of private equity, although most businesses fail before ever making it to the IPO stage.

For high-growth firms that reach the IPO stage and become publicly traded, post-IPO financing comes mainly from bank debt, new equity issues, and convertible bonds. This was the finding of a study of 367 firms that underwent an IPO in 1983, and the financing choices made by these same firms over the ensuing 10 years.[10] Within five years, many of these firms

were generating internal cash flows in excess of their investment needs, which means that they were generating positive
free cash flows.

Positive free cash flow indicates that the business has cash
left over after making its investments, cash it can then return to
the capital markets in the form of dividends, share buybacks,
or debt repayments. This is what we would expect, in time,
from any successful business. High growth should translate
into higher revenues, profits, and operating cash flows. But as
growth rates slow, which they must in all industries, companies
invest less aggressively than they had done in the heady days of
high growth. When moderation in capital spending is combined with increased operating cash flows, at some point these
cash flows exceed investment and external financing is no
longer required. Quite simply, achieving positive free cash flow
is one of the hallmarks of a successful, mature business.

But marketing to the capital markets is every bit as important for mature businesses as it is for firms that require more
external funding. It's just that the cast of characters changes.
Instead of targeting angels, VCs, and banks, most of the marketing effort is directed at the large institutions—including
mutual funds, pension funds, and insurance companies—that
hold the firm's debt and equity securities.

Special IPO marketing challenges are offered by so-called
microcap businesses—those companies with modest initial
market values (usually under $100 million, and sometimes far
lower than that figure). Recent years have seen the prolifera-
tion of mutual funds specializing in this category. But because
microcaps lack the market depth and liquidity of their large-
cap (i.e., high-value) counterparts, they are off-limits to most
large, institutional investors. In response, microcap companies

usually bypass the broker/dealer research departments of major players such as Merrill Lynch and Goldman Sachs, because such departments exist mainly to sell to large institutions. Instead, issuing companies go directly to the buy side. For example, one potentially successful strategy is to target professional money managers with growth-stock investment strategies, instead of so-called value investors. Another strategy is to court stockbrokers who cater to rich clients.

Given that there are so many other ways to raise growth capital, why bother going public in the first place? In addition to offering a convenient exit for earlier-stage investors, public companies enjoy an aura of respectability in the eyes of key corporate constituencies—such as customers and suppliers—that private companies struggle to match. Recruiting management talent may also be easier. For many entrepreneurs, there is no better proof that their company is world-class than a listing on the Nasdaq electronic market or on a major stock exchange. Such respectability can translate into more advantageous contracts, in addition to providing potentially valuable publicity.

But there are significant costs to consider. To protect investors, publicly traded firms are required to disclose financial information that usually goes far beyond what an entrepreneur would part with voluntarily. Producing this information and having it audited imposes further costs on the business. And the very process of going public is expensive. One important component of such cost is the underwriters' fee, which can run to 7 percent or even more of the issuing company's proceeds. The issuing costs alone are high enough to suggest that IPOs are probably not a logical step for companies that seek less than, say, $20 million in equity finance. Other approaches, such as private equity offerings (discussed in the next subsection), are usually more appropriate in such cases.

In the typical IPO, the shares are not bought directly by the investing public but rather by an investment bank (or often by a consortium of banks), which then uses its sales force to market the issue to investors. Underwriting is central to the IPO process, and few major IPOs proceed without it. The perceived advantage is that the issuing company is guaranteed a certain level of proceeds from the issue, regardless of how popular the shares prove to be with investors. But not only is the process costly, it is also confusing. Much of the confusion stems from the fact that there are different levels of underwriting services, some of which transfer market risk right back to the issuing company.

In general, underwriting can be "hard" or it can be "soft." The hard version is what most entrepreneurs and corporate managers think of when they envision their IPO. An investment banker buys the shares at a guaranteed price, and bears any risk should the issue fail to sell as expected. But this form of underwriting has become less common in recent years, and in certain parts of the world is practically nonexistent. In Southeast Asia, for example, only small, second-tier investment houses provide hard underwriting services. The large, U.S.-based banks nearly always insist on soft underwriting.

Soft underwriting is done on a "best efforts" basis, in which the bank underwrites a deal after the issue has been priced in the market. In other words, the underwriting occurs later in the process than under the hard version. The bank then places the shares with fund managers and other members of the underwriting syndicate (who proceed to place the issue with their own clients). Unlike hard underwriting, in which the bank might bear pricing risk for weeks, the deal is on the books for

159

no more than a few days, and sometimes for only a few hours. Even then, the bank might invoke force majeure clauses that allow it to avoid any risk should sales collapse just after the book-building process (during which the bank solicits interest from clients and other banks). To put it another way, the bank can often get out of the underwriting agreement in the event of natural disasters, riots, war, or labor strikes. Some contracts even allow redress for the banker if there are deemed to have been major political, economic, fiscal, or regulatory changes.

Soft underwriting has become controversial, in part because investment banks continue to charge clients a percentage of the proceeds. This practice is easier to justify with hard underwriting because of the risk that the banker takes on. But with a best efforts approach, the banks manage to lay off most of the risk back onto the issuing company. This has led some entrepreneurs and corporate executives to wonder why the banks do not charge by the day or by the hour. When there is little risk to the underwriter and fees are still charged on the basis of size, IPOs are a bonanza for the banks.

Firms must not only bear the direct costs of underwriting the issue, performing due diligence, and setting up adequate financial reporting systems, but they must also incur the costs of having key managers tied up for weeks in the grueling process of "road shows." Road shows, in which senior managers present their companies to the investment community, serve two purposes. First, they offer managers an opportunity to make a case to potential investors, particularly the large institutional investors, such as mutual funds, pension funds, and insurance companies, that have the most money to invest and that will ultimately determine whether the issue is a success. In addition, road shows help the investment bankers who manage the

issue to gauge investor demand. Bankers often have a reasonable idea of demand before the road shows even begin, but
face-to-face contact with key portfolio managers gives them a
better idea of how to price the issue.

To illustrate the demands that road shows can place on corporate managers, consider the case of Asiacontent.com, a Hong
Kong–based Internet content provider, when it went public on
Nasdaq in April 2000. The company raised $70 million (minus
$5 million in fees and expenses), down from an original target
of $106 million, but quite respectable given that Nasdaq had
just crashed. The CFO, CEO, and chairman made 80 presentations in 12 days, in such far-flung places as Hong Kong, Singa-
pore, Munich, Hamburg, Frankfurt, Milan, Edinburgh,
London, Los Angeles, Denver, Boston, and New York.[11]

Another important cost that senior managers and entrepreneurs should understand before going public is the well-
documented phenomenon of "underpricing." To illustrate, if
the offering price for an issue is $37 and the shares open for
trading at $45, the $8 difference is an implicit cost to the issuing company. Such underpricing has persisted for a long time,
and can be found on stock exchanges all over the world. For
the smallest issues (those under $3 million or $4 million), underpricing is typically 20 to 25 percent of the issuing price.
Even for issues in the tens of millions of dollars, underpricing
can be 10 percent or more.[12] Why this phenomenon has persisted for so long, and in so many markets, continues to be a
source of controversy and debate among finance professionals. But whatever the cause, the costs are real.

A study of more than 3,000 IPOs in the United States between 1990 and 1998 showed that the average IPO price was
14 percent below its first-day closing price.[13] For a typical IPO

in the sample, $23 million was left on the table by the issuer. Why do issuing companies accept this? One explanation offered by the authors of the study can be found in the notion that individuals value gains and losses of equal amounts differently. More specifically, they are risk averse in gains and risk seeking in losses, a finding well established among behavioral psychologists. On a practical level, this means that issuers become less concerned about each additional dollar the IPO can earn once they have determined that the offering will provide the necessary funding. Also, there is evidence that individuals mentally account for direct costs (in this case, the underwriters' spread) differently than they account for indirect costs (the underpricing, or the money left on the table). The authors argue that issuers do not push for higher IPO pricing because they place much greater weight on direct costs. This makes executives of issuing companies relatively complacent when it comes to underpricing.

In addition to an IPO organized by investment bankers, companies can also raise equity capital through a private placement or a direct public offering. For companies seeking relatively modest amounts of external equity, these are more logical alternatives than an IPO.

## Private Placements

In a private placement, the issuer sells directly to an investor, usually a large institution (e.g., a pension fund, mutual fund, or insurance company) that already holds a sizable block of the firm's shares or bonds. In the United States, if certain conditions are met, the SEC waives registration requirements, which significantly reduces cost and speeds up the process. The logic is that big, sophisticated investors can fend for themselves, and thus do not require the protections afforded to small investors by the registration process. For large issues, these savings can run into the hundreds of thousands of dollars.

Another important advantage of private placements over public offerings is that by targeting a small number of sophisticated investors, the issuer can structure a more focused transaction, one that appeals directly to those investors. Developing focused offerings is obviously harder in public offerings where, by necessity, a broader group of potential investors has to be appealed to.

Successfully pursuing this form of financing requires a basic understanding of applicable securities law and the procedural steps required by regulatory authorities, and at least some idea of which investors to target. In the United States, most private placements are filed in accordance with Rules 504, 505, or 506 under Regulation D of the Securities Act of 1933, with Rule 506 filings being the most prevalent. Rule 504 imposes the fewest restrictions but permits companies to raise no more than $1 million over a 12-month period. Rule 505 caps the issue at $5 million, while allowing sales to an unlimited number of "accredited" investors and up to 35 "nonaccredited" investors. Regulation D defines an accredited investor as one who meets qualifications in any of eight categories. For example, any person whose net worth (or joint net worth with spouse) exceeds $1 million qualifies, as does an individual with income in excess of $200,000 in each of the two most recent years or joint income with spouse in excess of $300,000 in those years. Directors and officers of the issuing company are also accredited, as are trusts with total assets in excess of $5 million.

Rule 506 imposes no limits on the size of the offering, and is thus the preferred choice for medium-sized and large companies. The main difference between this rule and Rule 505 is that any nonaccredited investors must be "sophisticated." A sophisticated investor is one who, while not falling into any of the categories required for accreditation, can reasonably be believed to have knowledge and experience in financial and business matters that render him or her capable of evaluating the merits and risks posed by the transaction. Any large institution, including mutual funds, pension funds, and insurance companies, would qualify as an eligible buyer under either the accredition rules or the sophisticated investor designation.

Not surprisingly, as institutional investors have grown in influence, so too has the importance of private placements. Traditionally, the major drawback to such investments was their lack of liquidity. But by the late 1980s the market had become large enough for investors to begin demanding a secondary market for trading these securities. The SEC adopted rules in 1990 permitting such trades. As a result, lack of liquidity is much less of a problem for investors than it used to be.

## Direct Public Offerings

There are equity finance alternatives to the traditional IPO and private placements. One example in the United States is the direct public offering (DPO), so called because the securities in question are issued directly by the company to the investing public without an investment banker acting as underwriter.[14] And, of course, without investment bankers there are no banking fees. DPOs are similar to private placements except that

164

the former have fewer restrictions on who the issuer can sell to. In keeping with the spirit of private placements, issuers are supposed to avoid unsophisticated investors. For all practical purposes, no such precautions are required for DPOs.

Direct public offerings have existed in the United States since the 1970s, and in 1989 the SEC simplified registration procedures for small companies wanting to raise funds in this way. The process was rarely used, however, until the Internet boom began in the mid-1990s. In a typical DPO, offering literature (the prospectus, etc.) is made available online, allowing investors to download subscription documents. If interested, they can then send a check to the issuing company. Of course, the subsequent collapse of Internet stocks has led to a sharp decline in the use of DPOs, but they still represent a valid option for companies that seek to raise modest amounts of capital through public securities markets.

DPOs are sometimes called "exempt offerings" because they are largely exempt from the lengthy registration procedures required for more traditional IPOs. However, the amounts that a company can raise in this way are tightly restricted. For example, an issuer pursuing a so-called Regulation A filing is limited to $5 million over a 12-month period. Issuers who file under the Small Corporate Offering Registration (SCOR) program are even more constrained, with a cap of only $1 million. Also, SCOR issues are possible only in those individual states that expressly permit them. The advantage of the SCOR program is that apart from audited financial statements, few formal requirements are imposed on the issuer. The process is quick and cheap. The hard part is convincing investors to commit funds to securities that are likely to have, at best, limited liquidity.

## NOTES

1. Anthony Saunders, *Financial Institutions Management: A Modern Perspective*, 3rd edition, Boston: Irwin/McGraw-Hill, 2000, p. 2.
2. Because they are of little relevance to business lenders, we ignore other types of depository institutions, such as savings and loans (S&Ls) and credit unions.
3. Saunders, *Financial Institutions Management*, p. 86.
4. Ibid.
5. For a discussion of additional benefits offered by financial institutions, see Saunders *Financial Institutions Management*, pp. 90–91.
6. Bryan Burrough and John Helyar, *Barbarians at the Gate: The Fall of RJR Nabisco*, New York: Harper & Row, 1990.
7. G. T. Sims, "Junk-Bond Defaults Rise in Europe, Outpacing U.S.," *The Wall Street Journal Europe*, July 18, 2002, p. A1.
8. S. Fidler and V. Boland, "Debt Mountains Threaten Avalanche," *The Financial Times*, May 31, 2002, p. 18.
9. U.S. Census Bureau, *Statistical Abstract of the United States: 2000*, p. 508.
10. J. Helwege and N. Liang, "Financing Growth after the IPO," *Journal of Applied Corporate Finance*, 1996, pp. 73–83.
11. S. Crane, "Road Warriors," *CFO Asia*, July 2000.
12. Roger G. Ibbotson, Jody L. Sindelar, and Jay R. Ritter, "The Market's Problems with the Pricing of Initial Public Offerings," *Journal of Applied Corporate Finance*, 1994, pp. 66–74.

13. T. Loughran and J. R. Ritter, "Why Don't Issuers Get Upset about Leaving Money on the Table in IPOs?" *Review of Financial Studies*, 2002 (Special Issue), pp. 413–443.
14. Although the discussion here focuses on equity finance, DPOs can also be used to issue bonds.

# PART THREE

# TOOLS FOR ATTRACTING AND KEEPING INVESTORS AND LENDERS

# 6

# Strategy: How to Win Investors' Mind Share

SEGMENTATION: VIEW YOUR INVESTOR
  CREATIVELY
    Role of Segmentation
    Segmentation Approach
    Effective Segmentation
TARGETING: ALLOCATING YOUR RESOURCES
  EFFECTIVELY
POSITIONING: LEAD YOUR INVESTORS CREDIBLY

Having examined the major sources of capital in the previous chapters, we are now ready to apply the theory and practice of marketing to help companies obtain cost-effective financing. Companies won't become effective by randomly knocking at the door of every funding source in the hope of opening one that will generously supply the required capital. A marketing mind-set can help companies in several ways. Marketing can help companies identify the best capital funders to approach. And the approach itself will need to be marketing-shaped. The company will have to position itself as a worthwhile investment in terms of its risk-return profile. The company's arguments for seeking finance must match the criteria of the particular funder. The company must effectively present its case on both a rational and an emotional basis. In receiving funding, the company must continuously communicate about its performance if it is to maintain investor trust. All said, a marketing mind-set will assist companies in finding good funding sources and winning their support, and then keeping it.

We present here the major marketing concepts to be used in this and the next two chapters. We will adopt the strategic business architecture of the Sustainable Marketing Enterprise Model.[1] This architecture has nine core *market*-ing elements, namely: *segmentation, targeting, positioning, differentiation, marketing mix, selling, brand, service,* and *process*. These nine elements are divided into three groups: strategy, tactics, and value. Strategy includes segmentation, targeting, and positioning. Tactics include differentiation, marketing mix, and selling. Value includes brand, service, and process. (See Figure 6.1.)

The role of the first dimension, marketing strategy, is to win consumers' mind share, in this case, investors. Segmentation is an analysis designed to distinguish between different groups of investors who have different needs, perceptions, preferences, and behaviors. After segmenting the investors into different groups, the company needs to decide which segments to pursue. This is called targeting. Targeting aims to allocate the company's efforts toward those groups of investors who are most likely to respond positively to the company's value proposition. This last element of strategy is called positioning,

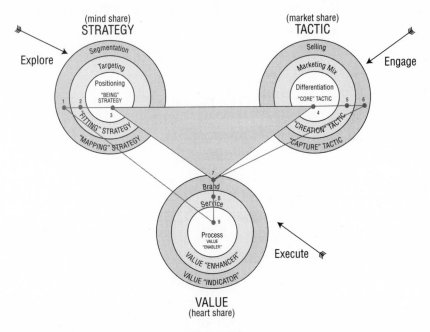

**FIGURE 6.1    The Strategy-Tactic-Value Triangle and Its Nine Core Marketing Elements**

173

which establishes the way in which the company wants to be seen by the target investors. After *mapping* (segmenting) the market and *fitting* (targeting) the company's resources into its selected segment, a company has to define its *being* (positioning) in the mind of the target market (investors) to have an attractive and credible position in their minds. (See Figure 6.2.)

## SEGMENTATION: VIEW YOUR INVESTOR CREATIVELY

Before a company can proceed with marketing, it must first establish what market and needs it wishes to serve. Its mission seeks to answer "What business are we in?" This should go beyond describing the products the company makes. It should

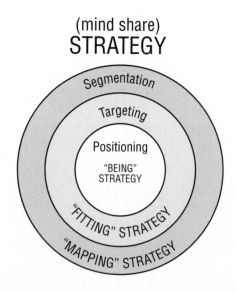

FIGURE 6.2   Strategy

describe the underlying benefits and services it wants to deliver to its target market. Thus the mission of Disney is to deliver family entertainment; Volvo wants to deliver safe transportation; and Xerox wants to improve office productivity. Amazon.com's mission, for example, is not simply to sell books, CDs, videos, toys, and consumer electronics but to "transform Internet buying into the fastest, easiest, and most enjoyable shopping experience possible—to be the place where you can find and discover anything you want to buy online."[2]

After deciding on its mission and market, a company has two basic approaches to attract funds from investors: to segment the capital market or to treat all capital market participants as potential investors. The latter is called *mass marketing*, meaning that the firm uses an undifferentiated marketing strategy in approaching investors. It views everyone as a potential investor. The traditional argument for mass marketing is that it creates the largest potential market for funding sources and simplifies and standardizes the appeal.

Few companies can benefit from a mass-market approach to investors. Considering the great diversity in capital providers' preferences in financing companies, a company will do better by segmenting the investor market. The company needs to divide the capital market into smaller segments based on similar characteristics, and then determine which segment is most likely to supply financing.

Segmentation serves as the primary strategic element in a company's marketing plan. It gives all other marketing actions a foundation on which to build a successful marketing strategy. By using segmentation a company can market more efficiently, targeting its marketing mix (product, price, place, promotion) program to those investors who are likely to be most receptive. Thus a biotech start-up firm would identify those venture capital firms that have been financing biotech firms and not waste its time approaching venture capital firms interested only in start-up firms in the electronics sector. Also, the company will know how to fine-tune its positioning and value proposition to the chosen target market.

Segmentation, the first element of strategy, can be defined as the process of partitioning the market into several groups of investors with similar characteristics who are likely to exhibit similar investment behavior.[3]

Consider the story of the Punch Taverns Group, a company that was assisted by Texas Pacific Group (TPG), a well-known private equity firm, in winning the European pub business.[4] To restore growth to Punch's pubs business, which had posted flat to declining sales for years, TPG helped it acquire Allied Domecq's 3,500 pubs, squaring off against a much larger suitor, Whitbread. In a deal that became the most hotly contested bid in Europe's private equity market, TPG and Punch successfully outmaneuvered Whitbread and won, in part by working Punch's balance sheet to lower the cost of financing the acquisition.

Texas Pacific Group was able to view the financing possibilities creatively by refinancing its original £1.6 billion bridging loan through securitizing its newly acquired pub assets. With the windfall of stable and predictable pub revenues, Punch isolated the rents it earned on real estate (a major source of cash flow for the company) and packaged them as real estate investment securities that could be sold to investors. In essence, TPG segmented the market for potential investors in Punch Taverns Group, separating assets (real estate) that would appeal to one class of investors, allowing it to focus on adding value to the pub business in ways that would appeal to other investor groups. This efficient capital structuring created savings of approximately £30 million in annual interest costs. The creativity of identifying this source of financing paid off in that Punch's pub revenues have been increasing at more than 7 percent annually, despite the maturity of the industry overall.

Segmentation is the *art* of identifying and pinpointing opportunities emerging in the capital market at a certain time. It is also the *science* of viewing the capital market based on geographic, demographic, psychographic, and behavioral variables. A company should be creative enough to spot a potential investor. It also has to clearly identify its potential investor from an advanced perspective using segmentation variables. Segmentation is a fundamental step that then determines a company's activities.

## Role of Segmentation

Segmentation is critical. First, it focuses a company's resources precisely where its value proposition matches investors' criteria. Second, segmentation is the starting point for developing a company's strategy, tactics, and value. Third, segmentation is the key factor in winning the competition for funds, by viewing a capital market from a unique angle and in a different way from its competitors.

Akamai, an Internet infrastructure success story, illustrates this point. Akamai was able to quickly accumulate the necessary funds, marked by its IPO in October 1999. The IPO occurred within a year after its first-round financing from Battery and Polaris Ventures. Akamai perceived that venture capital is not the sole source of funds. It recognized how potential players in the Internet industry (Apple, Cisco, and Microsoft) could become sources of funding and at the same time could be made into a profitable partnership to support a successful IPO.[5]

## Segmentation Approach

Several approaches can be used to segment a market. They can be categorized as *static attribute* segmentation and *dynamic attribute* segmentation.

Static attribute segmentation looks at similar, "static" attributes, which do not necessarily reflect investment behavior and do not directly influence an investor's decision to invest. This kind of segmentation includes the *geographic* and *demographic* types.

Geographic segmentation divides the market along geographical lines such as by region, country, province, state, or city. A company may decide to operate in one or only a few geographical areas, or to operate in all areas but pay attention to geographical differences in needs and wants.[6] This type of segmentation is one of the simplest methods for dividing markets into possible target segments. It usually serves as a framework for the other segmentation methods. For example, while a local entrepreneur would normally seek financing from local banks, angels, or venture capitalists, large multinationals logically seek financing from national or global debt and equity markets.

Demographic segmentation divides the market according to variables such as age, occupation, race, nationality, and education. This segmentation approach is especially suitable in seeking out individual investors—friends, family, and business angels. Even when demographic segmentation is not used as a primary segmentation tool, demographics are helpful in assessing the size of the target market and in reaching it efficiently.

Demographic segmentation can be supplemented by socioeconomic-based segmentation,[7] which can be based on income and social class. Corporate angels and entrepreneurial angels illustrate such segmentation. Corporate angels usually are former senior managers of large corporations who seek entrepreneurial investments in, say, the $100,000 to $200,000 range, and may also be looking for a senior management position. Entrepreneurial angels tend to be successful entrepreneurs who are looking for ways to diversify their portfolios. Their investments likely range from $200,000 to $500,000.[8] So it would be helpful if fund seekers would first gather this kind of information to better match their funding and management needs, instead of randomly approaching investors.

Dynamic attribute segmentation identifies attributes that reflect the human characteristics of investors—interests, habits, attitudes, and so on—that directly influence the investor's reason to invest. These include *psychographic* and *behavioral* variables. The first divides the market according to lifestyles or personalities. Investors in the same demographic group can have very different psychographic makeups. Consider John Sperling, a partly self-educated dyslexic and antibusiness tycoon, a left-wing academic who founded a for-profit university and who has spent most of his 80-plus years bucking convention. He is the kind of investor who will fund unpopular causes such as an anti-aging project, pet cloning, drug law reform, and saltwater agriculture. That attitude puts him squarely in the grand tradition of eccentric rich

Americans who use their wealth to pursue quixotic agendas, as was the case with Ed Bass, who built the infamous Biosphere, and Joe Firmage, the tech entrepreneur who funds research on aliens.[9]

Behavioral segmentation divides the market based on investor attitudes, responses, and benefits. Other behavioral bases used less frequently include perceptions, preferences, and marketing mix factors. A growing number of psychologists and behavioral economists have studied behavioral segmentation and have found some interesting facts about attitudes and responses to financial market conditions. Some of the most interesting are instant amnesia, arbitrary obsessions, fatal optimism, and compulsive monitoring.[10]

*Instant amnesia* refers to how quickly investors forget a bad experience. Look at the behavior of mutual fund investors in 2001. As markets continued to fall, some investors yanked their money out, withdrawing some $15 billion from stock funds in March, the largest monthly outflow in history. Then all it took was a 27 percent two-week Nasdaq rally in early April—capped off by a surprise 50-basis-point rate cut by the Federal Reserve—to reverse that. AMG Data Service estimates that investors plowed a net $5 billion back into stock funds between April 5 and April 18 alone. The history of financial markets is filled with similar episodes.

Investors with *arbitrary obsessions* tend to fixate on the price they pay for a stock. This can cause them to hold on to losers, or even worry about selling winners, based more on what should be random reference points than on the stock's intrinsic value.

*Fatal optimism* describes a condition in which investors convince themselves of whatever it is that they want to believe.

They give more weight to events that support their desired outcome than to contrary evidence.

Finally, people given to *compulsive monitoring* continuously check stock prices, with the result that they perceive greater risk. These investors are more likely to do something foolish, like sell a good stock in bad times. All said, these studies are useful in helping capital seekers understand the different behaviors of capital providers.

For a given market situation, there is no single best behavioral dimension. For example, banks have traditionally taken a long-term view of a company's prospects and management's ability to repay debt. By contrast, the fast-paced, fickle bond market can change its mind in an instant about a company's creditworthiness. But recently, many borrowers are finding that bank lending has come to resemble bond markets. Burned by costly lending decisions in the 1990s, banks increasingly look to the impatient and unforgiving public markets to guide them in how much to lend and on what terms.

In today's turbulent environment, creativity in carrying out segmentation is a key factor in beating the competition. The critical question is: How should an effective segmentation strategy be formulated?

### Effective Segmentation

Effective segmentation should display the following characteristics. First, the market must be viewed from a unique angle and in a different way from competitors. This enables firms to establish their own rules. If done right, and the size and funding capacity of the segments are big enough, a company can then drive its competitors into following its rules.

Second, the segmentation method must reflect investing behavior and determine the investor's reason to invest. For this reason, dynamic attribute segmentation is superior to the static attribute kind. Since this method leads directly to investing behavior, it can yield valuable information for decision makers in formulating a suitable strategy for influencing this behavior.

Geographic and demographic segmentation is naturally easier to perform, since accurate and precise data is readily available. However, this method of segmentation does not provide a picture of how, for example, investors choose to invest in (say) Microsoft instead of Oracle. Consequently, it is difficult to build a complete strategy incorporating positioning, differentiation, marketing mix, selling, service, process, and brand-building efforts.

Third, the targeted segments must be of significant size and have sufficiently good prospects for future long-term financing. The prospects need their characteristics described, so that positioning, differentiation, marketing mix, selling, and brand-building strategy can focus on these characteristics.

## TARGETING: ALLOCATING YOUR RESOURCES EFFECTIVELY

Having distinguished the major segments for potential funding, the next step is to evaluate them and determine which prospective investors to approach. This step is called targeting. It should result in a list of promising funding prospects ranked in terms of their likelihood to respond. Targeting aims to allocate the company's resources as effectively as possible.

A company should consider three criteria in determining

which segments to target. The first is that the target market segment is large enough. The second criterion is that the targeting strategy must be based on the company's competitive advantage. Competitive advantage is a way of measuring whether the company has sufficient strength and expertise to dominate or succeed in the chosen market segment. The third criterion is that the target segment must be based on the current competitive situation. General Electric's recent experience provides a good example of how companies can respond in creative ways to major industry, competitive, and macroeconomic change.

## POSITIONING: LEAD YOUR INVESTORS CREDIBLY

After carrying out segmentation and then targeting, you now need to position your company or offering in the mind of the investor. Here, the aim of positioning is to establish the borrowing firm's trustworthiness, confidence, and competence for investors—in a word, its credibility. As one observer defines it, positioning is the "reason for being."[11] The company must define its identity and personality in the investor's mind.

As we move more into the era of globalized markets, where capital can flow anywhere in search of the best returns, companies can no longer depend on their traditional investors to provide financing whenever it is needed. Borrowers can no longer "manage" their investors; their investors have to be "led." Leading takes credibility. Positioning, then, is not just about persuading. It is also about earning investors' trust and confidence.

183

How, exactly, do you set about obtaining trust? First, the capital-seeking firm must be seen to have competence in performing its business activities. Second, it must have a reputation for honesty in its use and sharing of information. And third, the firm must have a benevolent attitude toward the funding source, namely that it wants the funding source to do well.

On a day-to-day basis, the two parties must be open with each other. Louis Stern of Northwestern University's Kellogg School has cited the following six factors that contribute to two parties trusting each other:[12]

1. *Bilateral communication.* Both parties have equal input into joint decision making. They both listen to each other respectfully.

2. *Correctibility.* If there is any disagreement, there is an agreed-upon appeals procedure.

3. *Consistency.* The borrower follows the same policies, programs, and procedures that it originally outlined to the funder.

4. *Explanation.* If the borrower makes any substantial changes, it provides an explanation of why the changes are being made.

5. *Interactive justice.* At all times, the parties treat each other fairly and with respect.

6. *Local knowledge.* The borrower keeps the funder well informed about the borrower's situation.

Thus positioning aims to gain investor trust by making and keeping promises. Four criteria and their assessments will determine positioning: investor expectations, internal capabilities, competitors, and change.

The first criterion, *investor expectations*, means that the borrower must be perceived as capable of delivering an attractive risk-adjusted return. It's a well-worn axiom of capital markets that companies that cannot meet this criterion have no realistic chance of attracting financial resources at competitive rates.

The second criterion focuses on the company's *internal capabilities*. To illustrate this notion, consider the turnaround of Wesley-Jessen, formerly a Schering-Plough subsidiary. For years, Wesley-Jessen held on to a leadership position in specialty contact lenses, but lost its way in the 1990s. Looking to expand into larger markets, the company invested heavily in standard contact lenses, a segment in which it lacked both the expertise and the scale needed to succeed in that market. Worse, it also began to neglect its key customer base, the optometrists who wrote lens prescriptions. In time, Wesley-Jessen's management woke up and went back to basics. Its position as a company with great turnaround potential was soon realized by Bain Capital, a private equity investor. With Bain Capital's help, Wesley-Jessen raised the funding necessary ($100 million) to retool its standard lens factory to make specialty lenses. Within two years, Wesley-Jessen had achieved a total transformation in its business, culminating in a successful IPO in 1997.[13] Quite simply, its internal capabilities were positioned to appeal to venture capitalists.

The third criterion, *competitor assessment*, holds that a company's positioning should be unique and easily differentiated from its competitors. Considering Wesley-Jessen again: Returning to its uniqueness in making specialty lenses appealed to the capital market. Recognizing a company with turnaround potential in the contact lenses industry, Bain Capital was rewarded with the 45-fold return on its investment.

The fourth criterion, *change*, holds that a company's positioning must be relevant to conditions in its business environment. Positioning aims to plant a consistent perception, identity, and personality in the mind of the investor. Cereal maker Kellogg Company provides a good example. Realizing its position as a slow-growing company in a mature industry, it features dividend payouts, an essential differentiating element in its efforts to attract and retain investors. Its long-standing record of dividend payments has served as a bulwark against war and economic recession. In short, Kellogg has become the kind of company investors want to own if they insist on dividends.

Al Ries and Jack Trout, two pioneers of the positioning concept, said that the ultimate achievement of positioning is to "own" words or phrases in customers' minds. Sony, for instance, has a strong image for "innovation"; Wal-Mart has "everyday low price"; Volvo has "car safety." In marketing to the capital market, then, it is important to "own" words in the mind of investors, as Kellogg is associated with "steady dividends." These companies have achieved success because they have consistently used and sustained the same positioning statements for a long time.

## NOTES

1. The Sustainable Market-ing Enterprise Model has been popularized by Philip Kotler and Hermawan Kartajaya in

their best-selling book, *Repositioning Asia: From Bubble to Sustainable Economy*, John Wiley & Sons (Asia) Pte. Ltd., 2000, and *Rethinking Marketing: Sustainable Marketing Enterprise in Asia*, Prentice Hall, Pearson Education Asia Pte. Ltd., 2003.

2. See Philip Kotler and Gary Armstrong, *Principles of Marketing*, 9th ed., Upper Saddle River, NJ: Prentice Hall, 2001, p. 49.
3. See Art Weinstein, *Market Segmentation: Using Demographics, Psychographics and Other Niche Marketing Techniques to Predict Customer Behavior*, Chicago: Probus Publishing Company, 1994.
4. See Paul Rogers, Tom Holland, and Dan Haas, "Value Acceleration: Lessons from Private-Equity Masters," *Harvard Business Review*, June 2002, pp. 98–99.
5. Paul A. Gompers and Josh Lerner, *The Money of Invention: How Venture Capital Creates New Wealth*, Boston: Harvard Business School Publishing, 2001, pp. 63–64.
6. See Kotler and Armstrong, *Principles of Marketing*, p. 249.
7. Weinstein, *Market Segmentation*.
8. See Mark van Osnabrugge and Robert J. Robinson, *Angel Investing: Matching Start-up Funds with Start-up Companies*, San Francisco: Jossey-Bass, 2000, p. 85.
9. See "Inside the Very Strange World of Billionaire John Sperling," *Fortune*, April 29, 2002, p. 66.
10. Ibid., p. 108.
11. Yoram J. Wind, "Positioning Analysis and Strategy," in G. Day, B. Weitz, and R. Wensley, eds., *The Interface of Marketing and Strategy*, London: JAI Press, 1990.

12. See Louis W. Stern, "Dealing with Justice," an interview in *Routes to Market*, Spring 2002.
13. See Paul Rogers, Tom Holland, and Dan Haas, "Value Acceleration: Lessons from Private-Equity Masters," *Harvard Business Review*, June 2002, pp. 96–97.

# 7

# Tactic: How to Win Investors' Market Share

DIFFERENTIATION: INTEGRATING CONTENT,
CONTEXT, AND INFRASTRUCTURE

MARKETING MIX: INTEGRATING OFFERS AND
ACCESS

RELATIONSHIP SELLING: INTEGRATING COMPANY
AND INVESTOR

H aving employed segmentation, targeting, and positioning to develop a marketing strategy to win investors' mind share, tactics are then needed for winning investors' market share.

The first element of these tactics is *differentiation*. Differentiation is the *core* tactic and key to standing out from the competition and building superior mind share and heart share in the target investors. The second element is *marketing mix*, known as the *creation* tactic that integrates a company's offer and access. The third element is *selling*, often defined as the *capture* tactic for integrating investors with the company in a long-term, mutually satisfying relationship. (See Figure 7.1.)


## DIFFERENTIATION: INTEGRATING CONTENT, CONTEXT, AND INFRASTRUCTURE

As stated earlier, positioning is how a company wants to be seen by its target investors. Positioning has to establish the borrowing firm's trustworthiness, confidence, and competence—in a word, its credibility. To do this, positioning must be backed up by strong differentiation. When positioning is not supported by differentiation, the company may well overpromise and underdeliver, putting its brand and reputation at risk. In contrast, if positioning is supported by differentiation, that company will establish strong brand integrity.

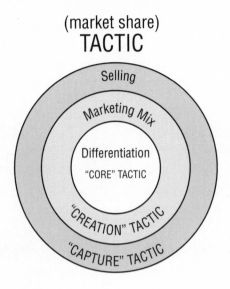

**FIGURE 7.1   Tactic**

Differentiation is a crucial factor for success in attracting company funding. In an influential article published in the *Harvard Business Review*,[1] Michael Porter concludes that strategy is essentially the creation of a unique positioning backed by a distinct set of activities. The essence of strategic positioning is to choose activities that are different from those of one's rivals. A company's sustainable competitive advantage will be developed through the "strategic fit" between the various activities that make up this unique position. Thus Porter assumes that positioning and differentiation are the key to achieving competitive advantage. They form the essence of a company's strategy and tactics. Positioning is the core of strategy, while differentiation is the core of tactics.

Traditionally, differentiation is defined as designing a set of

191

meaningful differences in a company's offerings. This definition is still valid. But we propose to go further, defining differentiation as "integrating the *content* (what to offer), *context* (how to offer it), and *infrastructure* (the enabler) of our offerings to investors"

Content refers to the value offered to investors. It is the *tangible* part of differentiation. Context is the way value is offered. It is the *intangible* part of differentiation, and relates to helping investors perceive an offering differently from those of competitors. The last, infrastructure, refers to the leadership, people, and facilities used to differentiate content and context.

As an example, consider Starbucks. (See Figure 7.2.) The market has dubbed Starbucks its "most admired food service company with a long-term shareholder value orientation." A study by the Hay Group puts Starbucks in *Fortune*'s Top 10 of

FIGURE 7.2   Starbucks: Content, Context, and Infrastructure

America's Most Admired Companies in 2003.[2] The company's credible positioning is backed by its solid differentiation.

Starbucks' differentiation can be readily identified using the three dimensions proposed. First take content. This is a unique specialty coffee company that is extremely profitable. Since it went public, Starbucks has successfully booked an annual sales and profit growth of 20 percent and 30 percent, respectively, hitting $2.6 billion and $181.2 million in 2001. The key to Starbucks' high profitability is from its success in recharacterizing drinking coffee as an experience, a considerable leap from being simply a commodity drink, and in taking it beyond mere goods and services.[3] Starbucks has cleverly repositioned coffee drinking, taking a centuries-old, very familiar experience and reformulating old and new aspects so it focuses on the mystique and enchantment that has always hovered around coffee over the centuries.

Second, consider differentiation by context. From the outset Starbucks has pursued investors who understand the company's overall values. This is to ensure that investors are not attracted only to the company's financial side, regarding its IPO as just that of another potentially profit-generating company. Starbucks hopes its investors will also value its nonfinancial aspects, such as the embraced values and enthusiasm of its people, and the company's vision and mission. Investors should view the package of company values as an indivisible whole.[4]

Third is infrastructure differentiation, the enabler of Starbucks' content and context. Starbucks' infrastructure incorporates two distinguishing aspects: its leadership and its people. The first is the stamp of Howard Schultz's leadership. Much of Starbucks' success, from its beginnings to its current global standing, is due largely to Schultz. Through his active participation in marketing Starbucks to the capital market, investors came to acknowledge Schultz as an innovator in the design of food services businesses.

In fact, Howard Schultz proved his integrity to the capital market from Starbucks' early days.[5] In March 1987, Schultz, who was then developing Il Giornale, his own coffee shop chain, had an opportunity to buy Starbucks from its founders. Given his financial position at the time, raising the nearly $4 million required was an almost Herculean task. Worsening the situation, he got news that one of his influential long-term investors was already making his own plans to buy Starbucks, which would heavily dilute not only Schultz's own ownership share, but also those of other investors who had put their trust in him. To prevent this move, he sought additional support from other investors. Fortunately for Schultz, his integrity in the eyes of other investors and his reputation for treating others with respect and dignity, including his employees, helped him to pull in the funds he needed to buy Starbucks. In fact, even Microsoft's Bill Gates invested in Schultz.

In later developments, Schultz recruited Howard Behar for his retail expertise and financial expert Orin Smith. The trio is now known as $H_2O$. Behar and Smith, with their long-standing experience as experts in operations and finance, balanced Schultz's energy, passion, and vision (but relative lack of management experience). This combination created strong credibility with investors. The second aspect of Starbucks' infrastructure differentiation is its people. The company's principle is that every Starbucks employee is treated as a partner.

This is reflected in paying higher wages than comparable companies and in giving health benefits to part-time workers. Starbuck's also established an employee stock option plan to align the rewards of employees and shareholders.

High-quality leadership and a large core of trusted employees form the infrastructure that has allowed Starbucks to differentiate its content and context. Without these attributes, the company's impressive record of sales growth would not have been possible.

Proper integration of differentiation, content, context, and infrastructure is required to ensure longevity. These dimensions must be compatible and interact to create the unique values that are the basis of the company's competitive strength. Starbucks' ability to differentiate led market players to believe in its future potential, and enabled the company to proceed with an astonishing worldwide expansion to more than 3,000 locations from 2000 through 2002. Effectively, this made Starbucks one of the world's fastest-growing brands (although growth declined in 2003, for a variety of reasons).[6] After it went public, its sustained average sales and profit growth meant, not surprisingly, that Starbucks' stock price performance in the 1990s outstripped that of General Electric, Coca-Cola, IBM, and many other blue-chip companies. With its proven long-term shareholder value orientation, Starbucks has successfully created a credible position in investors' minds.

In the sidebar, we describe another company, Berkshire Hathaway, which developed trust in its investors through managing the content, context, and infrastructure of its activities.

## Berkshire Hathaway: Winning Investors' Market Share

Berkshire Hathaway has always differentiated itself by claiming to be "the best at maximizing long-term shareholder value." (See Figure 7.3.) Given that a share price of $22 in 1965, shortly after Warren Buffett took over, grew to more than $60,000 35 years later, the claim is a credible one.

Consider how our three-dimensional model of differentiation helps us to understand Berkshire Hathaway's success. First let's first examine content. What distinguishes Berkshire's content is the unique value offered to its shareholders. Operations are highly profitable, and the company consistently generates huge amounts of cash flow. Berkshire Hathaway

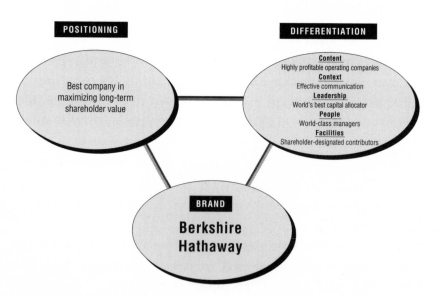

FIGURE 7.3    Berkshire Hathaway: Content, Context, and Infrastructure

has been especially astute in managing its insurance businesses, including the Government Employees Insurance Company (GEICO), the sixth-largest auto insurer in the United States, and General Re, one of the world's biggest reinsurers.

Second, consider Berkshire's context differentiation. The company's remarkable success in building and maintaining trust with investors through its annual report and annual meeting is particularly noteworthy. The annual report is designed expressly to be understandable for the average investor. The report is supplemented by an owner's manual setting out Berkshire's methods for selecting, managing, and valuing its businesses. Berkshire Hathaway's well-known annual meetings held in Omaha and popularly termed the "Woodstock for Capitalists,"[7] are also unique. Question-and-answer sessions with Buffett and vice chairman Charlie Munger have been known to last longer than five hours. How many corporate bosses are willing to show such patience and concern for their shareholders?

The third dimension, infrastructure differentiation, has three facets: leadership, people, and facilities. We consider the first two here. The leadership provided by Warren Buffett, supported by his colleague Charlie Munger, is key to Berkshire's success. The capability of these two has been tested and proven for more than 30 years, placing them among the world's best capital allocators. In over 30 of its first 37 years under Buffett, Berkshire's results have beaten the S&P 500, often by a large margin.[8]

Berkshire Hathaway is adept at recruiting and retaining the top talent in its industries. These people usually have established their capabilities before they come to Berkshire. They enjoy their work and thrive on performance. They think like owners and enjoy becoming engrossed in every facet of their business. This cadre, comprised of nearly 40 managers, is fiercely loyal and dedicated to Berkshire Hathaway. Few have ever chosen to leave. This fact alone reflects the company's world-class standing.[9]

Clear differentiation requires content, context, and a unique infrastructure. These three aspects must be properly integrated to create the unique values that form the basis of a company's ability to be truly competitive. In Berkshire Hathaway's case, shareholders have the longest investment horizon of practically any public company in the world. Most investors plan to die still holding its shares.

## MARKETING MIX:
## INTEGRATING OFFERS AND ACCESS

Marketing mix, the second element of tactics, can be divided into three types. The first is *destructive*. It neither adds customer value nor strengthens a company's brand. The second is *me-too*. It simply copies existing marketing mixes from others in the same business. The third is *creative*. This entails adoption of a marketing strategy (segmentation, targeting, positioning) and the other maxims of marketing tactics (differentiation, selling), and the building of marketing value (brand, service, process).

Marketing mix means integrating offers and access to investors. A company's offer of products and prices must be closely tied to access, consisting of places (channels) and promotions to attract investors. (See Figure 7.4.)

We now consider each of the four marketing mix elements and their applications to the capital market. The first element, product (in this case, the financial securities offered to in-

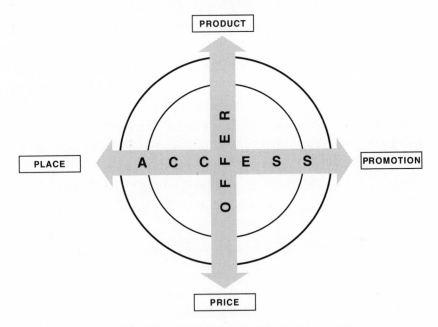

FIGURE 7.4   The Two Dimensions of Marketing Mix:
Offer and Access

vestors), is equity (shares) or debt (bank loans, bonds, leasing, etc.). As we noted in Chapter 5, many companies offer investors hybrid instruments that comprise both debt and equity components. Convertible bonds are one example; bonds with detachable warrants (a type of stock option) are another. Because of the capital market's unique and evolving demand—strongly affected by political and economic situations, such as with changes in the laws or statutes or a sudden jump in interest rate volatility—investors continue to demand new capital market products. Taking into account a company's stage of growth and its value creation capabilities, issuers (from entrepreneurs to established corporations), with the help of Wall Street, have customized their products to match investors' demands.

Wall Street plays a significant part in inventing new financial products that fit investor demands. The liquid yield option note (LYON[10]) is a striking example, one of the most successful financial products created in the 1980s.[11] In 1983, a Merrill Lynch options marketing manager cleverly identified the investment preferences of individual investors who were mostly risk avoiders, investing mostly in short-term government securities but willing to risk a fraction of their funds (just the interest income from these securities) in the highly risky options market.

Based on this perceived need, a complex new financial product—combining all the features of zero-coupon, convertible, callable, and putable bonds—was created, known as the LYON. It proved successful because it suited individual investors well, and also enabled funds seekers to tap retail market investors as a new source of funds.

Investor preferences for capital market products are often strongly affected by regulations, especially when it comes to institutional investors such as pension funds. Capital providers, from individual investors through to financial institutions, have their own preferences in selecting financial products for investment. Venture capitalists generally do not buy common stocks per se, as their investments in potentially high-growth companies mean also high risk. However, they do need to protect their investments from vanishing because next-round financing inevitably brings in new investors to replace them. Consequently, they do need financial products that ensure that an entrepreneur's stake cannot be finalized until the value promised to them has been met.

Three financial products that fit venture capitalists' preferences are frequently employed together with common stock. These are preferred stock, vesting, and covenants.[12]

Because of its liquidation preference over common stock, *preferred stock* is the residual claim after the venture capitalist has recovered the stock's purchase price. So venture capitalists hence ensure they recover their investment in the event of a forced sale or company liquidation. Preferred stock also allows venture capitalists to match reward with an entrepreneur's performance.

*Vesting*, on the other hand, does require an entrepreneur to stay with a company for a period of time, or until value has been realized, and the stock proportionately becomes his over that period. Vesting motivates entrepreneurs to achieve the value creation they promised to the venture capitalist and thereby to realize ownership.

The last method, *covenants*, is a legal agreement between the venture capitalist and the company. It is a basic form of protection that can be tailored to a specific issued concern by the related parties. It greatly depends on the negotiating power of the related parties. Most of these covenants are directed toward a greater involvement of the venture capitalist in controlling financial strategy, while the entrepreneur has more focus in determining operations policies.

The second element of marketing mix, price, denotes what investors must pay for what they buy. One of the capital market's distinguishing characteristics is that companies have only limited power to set the prices of their products, particularly in the public capital market. An issuer company—with its investment bankers—does have some room to maneuver in setting the price of stock before an IPO. After this happens, though, in mature markets at least, they can no longer exert much control over the prices of stocks or bonds. After going public, all that a company can do is to lead the market in the right direction through good communication and promotion.

Getting an IPO target price right is not straightforward. Substantial doubt on how the market overall will welcome the IPO will still exist, even after investment bankers' surveys. The set price must satisfy both investors and issuer. If it is too high, the IPO may fail to attract investors, because that price will be thought not to offer an appropriate return. On the other hand, should it be too low the IPO will not yield the optimum outcome in terms of funds raised. This, in turn, will affect the reputation of investment bankers sponsoring the IPO. This is why it is important to determine the right IPO price to ensure a continuity of capital-raising activities from the capital market.[13]

After the IPO, pricing behavior on the stock market will then emulate what happens in a perfectly competitive commodity market, where an industry player could only accept the market price. Supply and demand, and risk and return mechanisms will then determine the prices of a company's common stocks, bonds, and derivatives. These prices will depend on global and national economic climates, industry outlook, and, undoubtedly, the prospects for the company itself. A company's stock price volatility can now thankfully be limited—to a degree. By studying what causes stock price movement, a company can then tailor its promotion program to potential movers of its stock prices so it can then lead investors appropriately.[14] Should a company have sizable market capitalization and have backed this up with credible positioning and differentiation, it may then be able to influence potential investors, as occurs in a monopolistic, competitive commodity market.

Investors' way of assessing a price offers a useful tool to assess the reasonableness of the prices a company gets for its stocks or bonds. Intelligent investors assess reasonableness of a stock or debt price relative to the value that they get. In other words, they regard price as what you pay and value as what you get.[15] It is good if the price is equal to the value, what we call a fair price. But sometimes the facts tell a different story. When the price exceeds the value, we call the price "high." This is exactly what happened in the dot-com boom. There was, as Robert Shiller called it, "irrational exuberance."[16] When the reverse happens, the value is perceived to exceed the price, we call the price "low." And it won't remain low for long.

Product and price make a combination called an offering, which reflects the value that a company offers to an investor. To make value creation complete, access to the investor is needed. This involves the third and fourth elements of the marketing mix, namely place and promotion.

The third element, place, is where investors are able to search for the right companies in which to invest. Entrepreneurial companies usually use their business networks as channels to become known to the angels or venture capital communities.

Then, after a company wins its first financing, this angel or venture capitalist will usually act as the channel to let it progress to its next round of financing. This is how successful companies such as Apple, FedEx, Compaq, Amazon, and Akamai got a boost in their early stages of development. With their extensive networks, angel or venture capitalists can introduce entrepreneurial companies to their colleagues and to banks.

For the next financing round, these angels, venture capitalists, and banks can then support companies to get public funds from the capital market. After companies have already gone public, this channel will most likely be handed over to brokerage firms and institutional investors.

For the fourth marketing mix element, promotion, to be effective, it is important to select the right communication tools to raise awareness and aid recall with target investors. A range of promotional tools is commonly employed by capital market participants: personal selling, public relations (PR), and investor relations.

*Personal selling* develops buyer preferences, bolsters conviction, and leads to action.[17] This tool is generally more effective when a CEO becomes personally involved, as the capital market needs information from companies' foremost trusted and responsible persons. Jack Welch, GE's former CEO, for instance, staged many presentations, question-and-answer sessions, and road shows, just to convince the capital market of his company's performance.

*Public relations* can generally be a very effective promotional tool to raise capital. It has the advantage of credibility,[18] which stems from using independent third parties, who consider many more objectives than a company that is simply promoting itself. For start-up companies, PR is very useful in getting the capital market's attention and in generating excitement. A biotech start-up firm, for instance, developing new treatments and methods for cancer diagnosis,[19] should get a story about itself into *The Wall Street Journal* or should at least circulate its name among venture capitalists to generate excitement. This would help it in raising funding.

PR has also proved to be very beneficial for companies seeking to make a successful IPO. AsiaInfo, a Beijing-based Internet infrastructure provider, for example, is a good case study of how a company made a successful IPO, at least in part thanks to an integrated PR program by Ogilvy Public Relations Worldwide.[20] Held back by uncertainty, confusion, and the dearth of knowledge on the Internet market in China, investors found difficulty in making a reasonable assessment of the Chinese Internet company, even though it actually had very strong growth prospects. Hence, it was not easy for a company not known outside China to have a successful listing in the United States. It needed an integrated PR program to introduce itself to U.S. investors.

Before a PR program could be properly undertaken, corporate internal IPO education was held first, so AsiaInfo management really understood the difficulties that were likely to arise and could be helped through the PR program that had already been announced. Only then were its corporate brand and identity established and introduced, in line with its positioning as China's leading Internet infrastructure solutions and software company. Subsequently, interest in and understanding of AsiaInfo's products and services were shaped and promoted and continued through ongoing communication—a road show that began simultaneously in Barcelona, New York, and Hong Kong—to explain AsiaInfo's business model and its competitive advantages. The objective of all this was to ensure recognition and support from international media that would create interest, enthusiasm, and a positive reputation among capital market players—particularly industry analysts and institutional investors—with regard to AsiaInfo's future prospects.

The result from this integrated PR was clear from the success of the company's IPO, as offers jumped to twice what they had been (to $140 million), and on the first day share trading soared to 362 percent, one of the strongest IPO's that year.[21] This was of course inseparable from the success of AsiaInfo's PR, which it had undertaken jointly with the support of Ogilvy PR, where the company's solidity in a volatile market was mostly reported in leading international publications such as *The Wall Street Journal* and *Far Eastern Economic Review*.

After an IPO, PR will probably still be needed to stabilize share prices, the movements of which are strongly influenced by economic and political conditions, plus any negative issues that develop in the market. By communicating continuously with the media, for instance, during market downturns, a company can divert the focus from stereotyped evaluations to company fundamentals that are themselves actually still sound.

*Investor relations* are frequently used to update market players directly about the latest developments within a company. Considering the multitude of companies in the public capital market contending for funds, it is no surprise many have set up separate investor relations departments. By 1994, 56 percent of Fortune 500 companies already had their own.[22]

Investor relations are basically tasked with organizing investor events professionally, managing money manager relationships, and circulating important new information to investors. IBM, GE, Cisco Systems, and other blue-chip companies frequently use their investor relations departments and CEOs extensively to boost themselves in the capital market.

But in the current turbulent environment investor relations may need to take a more strategic role. CEOs must be comprehensively supported in anticipating the market's response to new strategies and other major policies.[23] The investor relations department must hence be able to accurately predict stock price movements. This is essential because falling stock prices could significantly increase the company's cost of capital, hindering acquisitions and mergers and simultaneously weakening employees' and customers' trust. The investor relations people must manage the key account process appropriately to guard against this, identifying major investors who could potentially affect stock prices, and then understanding their behavior.

Once access to the investor has been established through a certain place and promotion approach, all a company's offerings can be delivered smoothly to targeted investors. The tactic of integrating offer and access is then complete.

When Starbucks applied its marketing mix, its investment product was its common stock, considering its policy of minimal use of debt. The cumulative total return of its common stock over five years—ended 2002—has been superb, beating the Nasdaq market index by a wide margin.[24] Considering its long-term shareholder value orientation that demands investors look at the company as a complete package, not from only the financial side, Starbucks' stock price has been fairly reasonable—reflecting the company's performance, which has certainly been very strong—since its mid-1992 IPO.[25] Because of its incredible growth and respectable reputation, most capital market channels want to handle the stock, especially brokerage firms. Personal selling through its annual meetings and active public and investor relations have made for very effective promotion. All its marketing mix components have creatively supported differentiation in content, context, and infrastructure. In other words, through a winning combination of marketing mix elements, Starbucks has successfully brought about a dynamic differentiation that backs up its strategy.

## RELATIONSHIP SELLING: INTEGRATING COMPANY AND INVESTOR

The last element of tactics is relationship selling. The principle of relationship selling does not refer to personal selling of specific products to investors. What is meant is the tactic of creating long-term relationships with investors through their ownership of the company's financial products. It is the tactic of integrating company and investor. After developing strategy and creating a good differentiation and marketing mix, the company should be able to generate financial returns through relationship selling. This is the company's *capture tactic*.

Selling represents only one small stage of the whole relationship process. The act of selling should be preceded by proper sales planning, and followed by proper service and relationship management to guarantee the effectiveness and efficiency of sales efforts.

However, selling to the capital market is quite different from selling to customers. For one thing, selling to the capital market requires a company to sell the business fundamentals that are represented by its financial products. Secondly, buyers' motives are also different, because in normal sales situations buyers purchase for consumption, while in the capital market investors purchase for investment.

So how do these differences impact the sales process? First, buyers in the capital market tend to be more information hungry and more skeptical than buyers of, say, consumer goods. Also, because of the long-term nature of investments, a sale never ends with the transaction, because all sales are refundable. Capital market buyers have invested in a relationship with the company. For this relationship to work, the company must constantly reassure and update the investors on its vision, business prospects, financial viability, and profitability. When the company is not responsive, the capital market will quickly shift its attention to more promising investments.

If the selling process is to reach the right kind of investors, a company must first assess its own stage of development. It must then determine the range of value it considers important and that many capital providers can provide. For instance, in the depth-of-pocket category, nothing beats capital markets for their ability to repeatedly raise large amounts of money. Unfortunately, however, the process of going public is convoluted and expensive. This makes it best suited for established companies that need external capital to grow their business.

The most obvious form of selling to the capital market occurs in the earliest part of a company's life cycle, during the angel and venture capital phases. When the company and the angel investor or venture capitalist are separate parties with different needs and motives, the sales process usually involves much research, preparation, and planning. Of course, all sales begin with proper prospecting. As described under segmentation and targeting, resources must be focused on the most promising potential investors. The catch is that identifying these is difficult. Luckily, many venture capitalists and angel investors will state up front their goals and expectations.

Once a candidate who is highly likely to invest is located, he/she must be approached professionally. A customized oral (and maybe visual) presentation may need to be prepared to satisfy the investor's demands and main concerns. This should cover company vision, business prospects, financial viability, and profitability; but the real focus should be on the investor's needs. Is the investor looking for an annuity, short-term, or long-term return? Do they understand the industry and business model? What were their past investments? What are their main concerns about the company? These must all be researched before making a sales pitch to angel or venture capitalists.

Once these angel and venture capitalists are successfully

sold on the investment prospect, this relationship must then be expanded and deepened to incorporate mutual trust and collaboration. Investors must also be continually updated on the state of their investment, and their opinions and wishes must be respected. All this will reinforce their conviction of the investment's quality.

In the next stage of a company's life cycle, when financial capital is more commonly obtained from banks, the company will be viewed completely differently than it was by angel and venture capitalists. For one thing, banks are much more risk averse than these. Secondly, unlike VCs, banks are not looking for extraordinary returns. Hence, a presentation should instead focus on the company's long-term viability and financial stability. Banks will often also require assets as collateral. Having these will invariably assist the borrowing process, as a bank's perceived risk is lowered with a collateral guarantee in its hands.

Relationships with banks are mainly formal. Most entrepreneurs expect their relationship and trust with lenders will develop gradually in dollars-and-cents terms. Hence, at the beginning of a company's relationship with a bank, it is most unlikely to receive a large loan. However, with each borrowing cycle, a bank will increase its trust in the company, resulting in a progressive increase in loans.

So, with the right strategy and strong differentiation supported by a suitable marketing mix, a funds seeker can then be said to be fully equipped and ready to capture needed funding. A company must then actualize this through its relationship selling. As the relationship becomes stronger the company, in turn, finds it much easier to obtain needed funding.

## NOTES

1. Michael M. Porter, "What Is Strategy?" *Harvard Business Review*, November-December, 1996.
2. See www.fortune.com/fortune/mostadmired.
3. James H. Gilmore and Joseph B. Pine II, *The Experience Economy*, Boston: Harvard Business School Press, 1999, p. 166.
4. Source: Howard Schultz and Dori Jones Yang, *Pour Your Heart into It: How Starbucks Built a Company One Cup at a Time*, New York: Hyperion, 1997.
5. Ibid.
6. See "The Best Global Brands," *BusinessWeek* Online, August 5, 2002.
7. See Amy Kover, "Warren Buffett: Revivalist," *Fortune*, February 16, 2001.
8. Source: Berkshire Hathaway Inc., *2001 Annual Report*.
9. See Andy Serwer, "The Oracle of Everything Warren Buffett has been right about the stock market, rotten accounting, CEO greed, and corporate governance. The rest of us are just catching on," *Fortune*, November 11, 2002.
10. LYON is a trademark of Merill Lynch & Co.
11. Source: John J. McConnell and Aduardo S. Schwartz, "The Origin of LYONs: A Case Study in Financial Innovation," in Donald H. Chew Jr. ed., *The New Corporate Finance: Where Theory Meets Practice*, 2nd ed. Boston: Irwin/McGraw-Hill, 1999.
12. See much more discussion of this matter in Paul A. Gompers and William A. Shalman, *Entrepreneurial Finance, A Case Book*, New York: John Wiley & Sons, 2002, p. 292.

13. See Roger G. Ibbotson, Jody L. Sindelar, and Jay R. Rittler, "Initial Public Offerings," in Chew, ed., *The New Corporate Finance.*

14. See Kevin P. Coyne and Jonathan W. Witter, "What Makes Your Stock Price Go Up and Down," *The McKinsey Quarterly,* No. 2, 2002.

15. The value here mean the intrinsic value of business, which can be defined simply as the discounted value of the cash that can be taken out of a business during its remaining life.

16. For further explanation see Robert J. Shiller, *Irrational Exuberance*, Princeton: Princeton University Press, 2000.

17. Philip Kotler, *Marketing Management: The Millennium Edition*, Upper Saddle River, NJ: Prentice Hall, 2000, p. 565.

18. See Al Ries and Laura Ries, *The Fall of Advertising and the Rise of PR*, New York: HarperBusiness, 2002, p. 85.

19. See "Climbing the Helical Stair Case," *The Economist*, March 27, 2003.

20. Source: www.ogilvypr.com/casestudy/admin/showtime7.cfm?num=193&headtop=3.

21. AsiaInfo's IPO was in March 2000.

22. See Graham Dowling, *Creating Corporate Reputations: Identity, Image and Performance*, New York: Oxford University Press, 2001, p. 146.

23. See an in-depth discussion of this topic in Kevin P. Coyne and Jonathan W. Witter, "What Makes Your Stock Price Go Up and Down," *The McKinsey Quarterly*, No. 2, 2002.

24. See: *Starbucks Corporation Proxy Statement for the Annual Meeting of Shareholders*, March 25, 2003.

25. Source: Yahoo! Finance, Historical Prices—SBUX (Starbucks Corp.) as of March 24, 2003.

# 8

# Value: How to Win Investors' Heart Share

BRAND: AVOIDING THE COMMODITY TRAP

SERVICE: AVOIDING THE DISSATISFACTION TRAP

PROCESS: AVOIDING THE FUNCTION-ORIENTATION TRAP

A fter identifying the needed strategies and tactics, the last dimension of the architecture submodel, value, can now be examined. (See Figure 8.1.) The aim is to win investors' heart share. The first element of value is *brand*, which is a company's *value indicator*—enabling it to avoid the commodity trap. The second element is *service*—ensuring a company meets or even exceeds investor's expectations. Service is often termed a company's *value enhancer*. The last element is *process*. This is a company's *value enabler*—enabling it

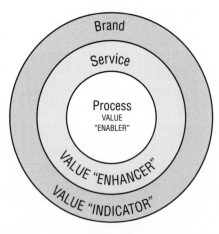

VALUE
(heart share)

FIGURE 8.1    Value

to deliver value to investors through various processes, both internally and externally.

## BRAND: AVOIDING THE COMMODITY TRAP

When positioning and differentiation are determined and supported through a solid marketing mix and selling strategy, a brand is the result. The brand is not developed solely through countless commercials in the mass media, or by applying a marketing mix. More importantly, it can be developed through applying the right strategies, tactics, and value.

Brand is not simply a name, logo, or symbol; nor is it merely the representation of a company's products or services. In the context of marketing to the capital market, brand is the "canopy" that represents a company as a whole—brand in this sense is more closely related to corporate brand. It is a reflection of a company reputation—value given and/or promised to investors. Hence, it is generally taken as a company's *value indicator*.

For the capital market—especially for financial analysts—a company with a strong brand is taken to be less risky than one with a weak one. So, a brand works in the same way for the capital market as for commercial ones; it reduces risk. A promise of a positive return and the reduction of risk are factored into stock/bond prices and other expenses. Near-certain future cash flows can then be assured, as General Electric virtually achieved over the past decade, missing just one analysts' consensus estimate in all that time.[1]

In this context, value is then defined as "total get" divided by "total give." Total get itself essentially has two components: *functional benefit* ($F_b$) and *emotional benefit* ($E_b$). Total give also has two components: *cost* (C) and *other expenses* ($O_e$). This is summarized in the value formula:

$$Value = \frac{F_b + E_b}{C + O_e}$$

A functional benefit comes from an attribute of an investment product that provides investors with functional utility. It usually relates directly to that product's basic functions for investors. With common stock, for instance, this functional benefit might well be stockholders' control over company affairs in voting to elect the board of directors and also the potential return from the dividends and stock appreciation. An emotional benefit is based on an investment product that provides emotional utility, like feeling safe when investing in Kellogg, or feeling excited when investing in Starbucks.

The cost is the formal toll to the investor in making the investment, and is usually embedded in the price of the investment product. As explained in previous chapters, because of so many inherent risks in raising capital, differences do occur in the cost incurred by purchasing the investment product relative to its perceived fair value, both before and after an IPO. Besides these costs, investors could later be burdened with other expenses—the cost of new funds needed to maintain ownership in the company, plus the cost of monitoring.

From this discussion, it can be concluded that a brand's strength is determined by these four components: Strong brands are marked on one side by high functional and emotional benefits, and on the other by low cost and other expenses, resulting in the largest possible "total get"–"total give" ratio. This formula also indicates that a company must do its utmost to yield a higher "total get"–"total give" than its funds-seeking competitors.

Brand is a firm's equity that adds value to the products it produces and at the same time to the investment vehicles it offers. A strong brand gives investors more confidence in the level and probability of a desirable return. A strong brand grants the firm some leverage over the perceived value of its investment vehicles. The Coca-Cola Company is thought to be worth $48 billion today, although it owns zero inventory.[2] Unfortunately, macroeconomists often fail to realize the power of brand as a price influencer. Brand frees a company somewhat from the commodity trap.

So it is important for a company to have brand equity. David A. Aaker's simple model of brand equity can be very useful in this context. He defines brand equity as "a set of assets (and liabilities) linked to a brand's name and symbol that adds to (or subtracts from) the value provided by a product or service to a firm and/or that firm's customers."[3] In marketing to the capital market this means the firm's investors. To have brand equity that generates value, a brand—as a company asset—needs investment to build up brand awareness, brand association, perceived quality, and brand loyalty.

First, *brand awareness* relates to the strength of a brand's presence in the investor's mind. Its levels range from simple recognition, to recall, to top of mind, and ultimately to dominance. Gaining this awareness with investors can well enhance brand equity, especially to be remembered for the right reason. Ogilvy PR's attempt at creating brand awareness of KPN Qwest—separately from its parent companies—serves as a good example of how brand awareness can help companies to raise funds through an IPO.[4] Through an integrated public relations program, KPN Qwest achieved strong awareness among the media and investment community who recognized it to be a leading brand in the Internet service provider industry. Thus KPN Qwest gained capital market acceptance, culminating in a successful IPO in 1999.[5] Its stock price jumped 31 percent on the first day of trading.

Second, *brand association* may include anything that relates an investor to the brand. It could take the form of investor imagery, product attributes, organizational associations, a celebrity spokesperson, or symbols.[6] Brand association is usually advanced through a brand identity program that shapes the development of this in consumers' and investors' minds. It is important to develop and apply a brand identity program to create high brand equity. A frequent mistake is to have a narrow focus on only the functional benefit attributes of products. Development of brand identity ought to be supported by the promotion of emotional benefits by making best use of various concepts of brand identity, such as brand as organization, brand as person, and brand as symbol.

Mature giant companies such as Kellogg and Ralston Purina have long been known for their relatively stable increases in stock performance (functional benefit) in the view of investors. As well, their level of earnings growth of between 10 and 12 percent annually for more than three decades, which is also bolstered by their consistent dividends paid throughout wars and recessions, provides investors with a feeling of security (emotional benefit).[7] The positive associations of these two brands, which are just what are hoped for, can be said to be quite a strong incentive for conservative investors to invest their capital in Kellogg and Ralston Purina.

Third, *perceived quality* is the special type of association that investors mostly buy. It is a bottom-line measure of the impact of brand identity.[8] It can also influence brand association in many contexts, especially when it serves as the key positioning dimension for corporate brands like Starbucks and Toshiba. It is impossible to have a perception of good quality without backing the claim with the real thing. To be able to offer good quality to investors, the true meaning of quality for them must be understood, using the value formula that was explained earlier. But this in itself is still not enough, as it is still necessary to shape perceptions.

Differences between perceived and actual quality may occur because investors may well not know the best way to evaluate the quality of a company, as in the case of Enron. Apart from that, investors also rarely have all the needed information to rationally and objectively determine a company's quality. Even though the necessary information is available, investors may not have sufficient time and/or motivation to process it cautiously.

As a result, investors tend to rely on one or two indications that they associate with quality. It is these indications that must be understood and managed by the company as the key that can be used to influence perceived quality. For instance, in granting loans banks place heavy emphasis on financial ratios as measures of the company's quality, so the company must ensure that its financial ratios fulfill these requirements.

Fourth, *brand loyalty* plays a key role as an indicator of brand value. It can ensure that a company gets funding and can act as an entry barrier to competitors because existing loyal investors are better positioned to respond favorably to changes in a company's operating and financial conditions. It is also less costly to retain investors than to win over new ones. So companies should not make the mistake of enticing new investors while neglecting existing ones.

For instance, one loyal investor in Wellman Inc.—a producer of polyester and nylon fiber—promptly committed to provide almost half the financing needed, even though at the time the company was leveraged so highly that major rating agencies would have placed it out of investment grade. Even better, this investor proved willing to release collateral on its existing holding. Given those terms of financing it was relatively easy to market Wellman to prospective investors. As a result, the company obtained new loans at a very competitive cost compared to the funds it had collected earlier.[9]

So, to ensure that it has a strong brand, a company must invest in and properly manage the four main dimensions of brand equity, that is: brand awareness, brand association, perceived quality, and brand loyalty. As a value indicator, a strong brand reflects investors' willingness to invest and also frees a company from the commodity trap. Thanks to its famous characters like Mickey Mouse, Donald Duck, and a host of other animation figures—the essences of which have been captured in its theme parks, in films, and by merchandisers—the Walt Disney Company is a very good example of how a strong brand frees a company from the commodity trap, as is evident from the following example.

Opened in the early 1980s, Tokyo Disneyland was unique because Disney held no direct ownership interests.[10] Through a 50-year license agreement, the company granted a license over the characters, technology and management skills that it had to Oriental Land Corp. In return, Disney receives 5 percent of the gate admission and 10 percent of all merchandise, food, and beverage sales. Such a deal could be made only by a company with a very strong brand—of the class of Disney.

With this strong brand Disney was also able to raise capital through a new investment product called *brand monetization*. An investment product was developed based on the right to receive a fixed amount of future royalties over a 20-year period as part of what Disney would receive through the Tokyo theme park. Through this mechanism Disney management hardly needed to guarantee anything in its own name. The investor was obliged to evaluate for itself the risks based on the strength of the brand and the possibility of a major earthquake occurring that would destroy the park or temporarily close it. Under these terms, any shortfall below the projected royalty stream would be fully carried by the investor. But any surplus above the annual amount would be received in its entirety by Disney.

This transaction created a unique record in the international market that remains unsurpassed, with the longest level of maturity and in the largest amount as well as the closest spread ever adopted. The total proceeds as of 1997 amounted to 90 billion yen—approximately $725 million. One of the senior executives of the largest participant in the underwriting group from a leading Japanese bank that handled this transaction summarized why they undertook the transaction: "Mickey Mouse is a better risk than the U.S. government." This proves again that a strong brand does free a company from the commodity trap.

## SERVICE: AVOIDING THE DISSATISFACTION TRAP

The second value-creation principle of a company is service. It can act as a short-term as well as a long-term *value enhancer* for a company's offerings. From the value equation, service means all the efforts to add value for investors by enhancing a company's functional and emotional benefits and reducing price and other expenses. In the context of capital raising, service to investors is reflected in the answers to such questions as:

- When there is a problem in the company's earnings forecast calculations in its financial report, does the company then resolve this and quickly inform investors?
- Does the company supply information about its strategies and future plans in a timely and reliable manner when requested to do so by the capital supplier?
- Does the company provide analysts with sufficiently comprehensive financial data to create an accurate valuation for investors?
- Does the company convey an impression of real willingness to act as a partner with the capital supplier?

To cope with competition for funds, a company must give investors service by continually enhancing its value to them. A classical model developed by Valerie Zeithaml, A. Parasuraman, and Leonard Berry can be taken as a set of guidelines for offering excellent service to investors.[11] Based on the model, a service must meet five general dimensions that represent the

222

criteria customers/investors use to assess service quality: tangibles, reliability, responsiveness, assurance, and empathy.

The first dimension, *tangibles*, refers to the appearance of a company's facilities, its financial reports, personnel, its business leader, communications material, and so on. In 2000, for example, Shell impressed shareholders with its annual report featuring an illustration that showed how it had simplified its overall corporate strategy in what it called its Sustainable Development Management Framework (SDMF). Through this simple framework Shell was able to easily and clearly explain to and convince investors about how it created value for shareholders and at the same time created wealth for society.[12]

*Reliability* reflects a company's ability to perform a promised service dependably and accurately. This dimension of service is very important, considering company-investor relations are always inseparable from the requirement to report the company's condition to investors, and that this reporting requires data accuracy. Reporting that is backed up by accurate data makes it possible for investors to make speedy and appropriate decisions connected with their investment. Hence, it is not surprising that many companies adopt various ways of enabling their investors to obtain accurate and reliable data.

Take the example of Irex Corporation, a public but closely held Lancaster, Pennsylvania–based company, the United States' largest mechanical insulation contractor and a leading insulation and acoustical materials distributor. During its private debt issue in 1992, the company provided a comprehensive offering memorandum to a carefully targeted group of private investors. The institutional investor that ultimately purchased the company's notes was given substantial detailed information. This investor met with senior management at the company's headquarters and learned about its leading market position, its business diversification, and its potential growth opportunities. He was also given enough information to allay concerns about a pending lawsuit that almost certainly would have put off public debt buyers.[13]

The third dimension of service is *responsiveness*. This is a company's readiness to help investors. These initiatives to assist investors can take various forms, including having a continuous one-to-one relationship to know investors' problems and interests, to quickly respond to the problems and complaints an investor faces, or to facilitate investor access to needed information connected with the company.

The Coca-Cola Company is one such example of a company that always pays attention to and helps its investors by establishing one-to-one relationships, particularly with its major investors or analysts. This company, for instance, gives special presentations to its major investors in the various conferences that it holds, such as at the 2003 Goldman Sachs Global Consumer Product Conference or at the Credit Suisse First Boston (CSFB) Global Beverages and Tobacco Conference. Periodically, Coca-Cola also hosts several discussions with targeted investors and analysts. Apart from that, it also periodically discusses financial performance in a webcast that investors can access on the Internet.[14]

The fourth dimension is *assurance*. It is about a company's trustworthiness and honesty to its shareholders. It is about how it delivers information transparently and honestly. It is about possession of the required skills and knowledge to perform the service it delivers. It is about how it makes its shareholders feel secure about owning company stock or bonds. And finally, it is about how the company's reputation is built up among investors. Honesty and the company's reputation have now become very important and are the main priorities of various companies after the accountancy scandals that brought down top companies such as Enron, WorldCom, and Global Crossing.

The WorldCom case is possibly the one that is most interesting, reminding us all how a strong company can be shattered in a relatively short time only because of dishonesty and a loss of credibility in investors' eyes. WorldCom was the second-largest U.S. telecommunications carrier, and it previously had been powerful enough to acquire MCI, a telecommunications giant that was its closest competitor. WorldCom spent more than $3.8 billion on routine expenses in running its business. But instead of reporting this as a cost of doing business, the company treated this money as being spent to buy assets, such as real estate and IT equipment. WorldCom then spread this cost over several years, allegedly making its profits (before taxes and other charges) appear to be $3.8 billion higher than they really were. The reputation and credibility of this company set up by Bernie Ebbers were totally destroyed. Its share price, which had hit $64.50 at its peak, quickly slumped to just 83 cents.[15]

And the last dimension of service is *empathy*. Empathy means that a company must endeavor to know its investors and their needs. By knowing shareholders' needs and expectations, a company will know how to serve and fulfill them. These efforts to understand shareholders are usually made by involving them in the reporting process or through one-to-one relationships and intensive communication.

To be able to give good service to investors, a company should enhance value using the five service dimensions just described. The case study following this on Royal Dutch/Shell's reporting approach and how that company runs its relationships with its shareholders and other stakeholders will deepen the understanding of how a company ought to improve its service based on the five dimensions of service.[16] The Royal Dutch/Shell Group of Companies was established in 1907 and it still dominates the oil industry, operating in more than 135 countries and employing around 96,000 people. It has become one of the world's richest corporations, with annual revenues far above the gross domestic products of many nations.

The oil industry is one that is very sensitive to social and environmental issues. Companies in the industry have come under pressure to acknowledge the wider responsibilities to take into account not only the interests of their shareholders, but also those of a much broader group of other stakeholders affected by their operations—employees, local communities, customers, and society at large. Responding to these increasingly stronger urgings from stakeholders, in the mid-1990s the company undertook a vast corporate transformation program.

Shell began to take a look at itself, questioning all fundamentals: its structure, the way it did business, the quality of its leadership, and its vision of the future. One of the fundamental changes made was that Shell applied itself to taking on new roles and responsibilities, not only in its industry, but also in society at large. It embodied these new responsibilities in its Statement of General Business Principles, which it revised in 1997 to include support for sustainable development and human rights.

In 1998, Shell published its first full-scale public report—*Profits and Principles: Does There Have to Be a Choice?*—which detailed the company's performance against its new business principles. In *Shell Report* 1999, it published details of its new management system—the Sustainable Development Management Framework—that it developed to create long-term shareholder value and brand strength while living up to its business principles and meeting society's expectations. And in *Shell Report* 2000, as mentioned earlier, the SDMF framework appears within a broader model that illustrates its role in creating value for shareholders and at the same time creating wealth for society.

The key to success in putting this concept into practice lies in Shell's success in measuring and monitoring the value it creates, the sixth stage in the SDMF framework wheel. Hence, to monitor and measure its performance in the context of sustainable development, Shell developed key performance indicators (KPIs) across triple bottom lines: economic, environmental, and social performance. In preparing these KPIs, Shell fully involved its stakeholders in conformity with the new business principles that it had embraced. In this process, Shell held 33 meetings with stakeholders, systematically recording, analyzing, and categorizing their input using well-defined KPI screening criteria. It also involved shareholders in the KPI exercise, including two large institutional investors as well as a number of other distinctive stakeholder groups such as nongovernmental organizations (NGOs), labor organizations, academia, and government. Shell has said it will continue this stakeholder dialogue as it develops the KPIs further.

Shell's approach in developing its KPIs makes a clear statement about what transparency really means to the company. To this company, transparency is an ongoing conversation with shareholders and other stakeholders. Transparency means more to them than just pumping out information in the hope of influencing stakeholders; it is fundamentally about allowing stakeholders access and engaging them. Shell turns information exchange into a true dialogue by engaging in two-way communication directly with stakeholders, severe critics included, through a variety of media.

One example of this dialogue is in its sustainability report. This includes "Tell Shell" response cards that invite comments, both positive as well as negative, from readers. Then it presents a representative example (praise and damnation) in the following year's report. Apart from that, Shell runs discussion forums on its web site that attract live and lively uncensored debate on hot topics from human rights issues through to global climate change.

This Shell case shows just how it pursues open dialogue through its annual *Shell Report* and on its web site. Through these initiatives, Shell demonstrates that it is one of the corporate leaders in transparency. Tom Delfgaauw, Shell's vice president of sustainable development, sees that Shell's future challenge is primarily to make sustainability a reality throughout all of its business. Shell acknowledges this will need a continuing cycle of engagement with stakeholders, uncompromising commitments to goals, open and honest communication about results, and reengagement for the future.

If all this is linked to its efforts to offer shareholders and other stakeholders excellent service, how does Shell then fulfill the five dimensions of service discussed earlier? First, Shell has been able to simplify its overall corporate strategy—Sustainable Development Management Framework—using a simple chart that is easily grasped and clear so it facilitates shareholders' understanding of its strategies and future planning. This means that Shell has met the first dimension of service, tangibles.

Second, in establishing its KPIs, Shell fully involved the shareholders and other stakeholders. These KPIs will be used to measure and report on Shell's progress in meeting its commitments to sustainable development. By fully involving the stakeholders, the KPIs obtained will be accurate and reliable so stakeholders, too, will be convinced that the strategies being pursued can be achieved by applying the KPIs. This means that Shell has met the second dimension of service, reliability.

Shell has also met the dimensions of responsiveness and empathy because it has taken a stance on information exchange between the company and its stakeholders as a true dialogue through two-way communication. It has also given stakeholders the opportunity to offer comments both positive as well as negative through its "Tell Shell" response cards. Apart from that, it has also held discussion forums on its web site to invite stakeholders to discuss openly various important issues faced by the company.

And finally, Shell has also provided assurance to its stakeholders because it has placed transparency as one of the most important components of its reporting approach. For instance, it has asked respected independent organizations to verify its publication of data. As the *Shell Report 2000* said, "Beyond assuring accuracy and reliability, verification increases stakeholder confidence that what is being reported is a fair picture of performance." In that report, KPMG and Pricewaterhouse-Coopers verified a range of performance data and statements on management systems and processes across the triple bottom line: economic, environment, and social performance.

## PROCESS: AVOIDING THE FUNCTION-ORIENTATION TRAP

The last value-creating principle is process. This is how a borrower effectively manages its capital-raising process to achieve its funding goals. Through effectively managing the activity chain in raising funds, a company will be able to achieve three objectives, namely to acquire quality investors (ones with good reputations, proven investing capabilities, and long-term vision); second, to keep the capital-raising cost as low as possible; and third, to get the funds it needs as quickly as possible.

It goes without saying that these capital-raising processes for the various funding alternatives (stock, bonds, bank loan, etc.) will have different stages, so the steps to manage them must also be different. For stock, for example, raising funds may be divided into three main stages: pre-IPO, during IPO, and post-IPO. Pre-IPO activities may include fixing the company's existing strategy, formulating a long-term financial strategy, creating company awareness and reputation among the investor community, selecting an investment bank as underwriter, and preparation for regulatory filing.

Activities during the IPO may include undertaking due diligence, preparing and conducting a road show, determining the IPO's appropriate price, and marketing the offering such as by circulating the prospectus to prospective investors. And finally, post-IPO activities may include maintaining relationships with investors and analysts and complying with regulatory body (SEC) requirements such as providing timely quarterly reports and conforming with the reporting standards defined by the SEC.

In broad terms, these capital-raising processes can be divided into three generic activities: *routine service delivery, handling investors' complaints,* and *new product development.* The first category is all those routine activities the company carries out to serve investors and analysts, especially at the post-IPO stage, such as in providing information and delivering quarterly reports for investors. Complaint handling is all those activities connected with appropriate management of investors' complaints. In many cases these are very important; remember that an error in managing complaints can often have fatal consequences in the form of a sharp drop in the stock's price in the market. Third, new product development activities are those that create new financial products and instruments to meet the company's and investors' needs.

The case that follows illustrates how one company managed all these activities efficiently and effectively.[17] In 1991, Comdisco Inc., a Chicago-based high technology leasing company, was interested in lowering its cost of funds. The process started with analyzing the situation in the capital market at that time. Financial services companies then faced a weak market, marked by collapses in the real estate market, the Middle East crisis, and a declining economy. A-rated bank debt traded at between 400 and 500 basis points over comparable Treasury yields. Only six transactions for financial services issuers rated below A were completed between September 1990 and April 1991, with the average credit spread at 240 basis points over Treasuries.

The company then needed to identify an appropriate financial product to issue in that market. Comdisco found an opportunity to lower its cost of funds by refinancing its short-term debt with the intermediate-term variety. The next step was to decide whether there were any available alternatives by which it could sell its senior notes fairly, given the weak state of the public market. Fortunately, it found a private market that would give this fairer consideration.

During its offering process, company management had to identify the most effective method to communicate with investors. Considering the overwhelmingly negative climate for financial services issuers, they had to use a personal, direct, and interactive approach in order to dispel the general concerns of most investors at that time. The most appropriate way was to use presentations to give potential investors the opportunity to thoroughly review the company's lease portfolio, particularly its excellent residual experience.

Handling all this well paid off handsomely; Comdisco's private issuance of three-, four-, and five-year notes was well received by investors. The company sold $100 million of senior notes to eight investors at credit spreads of 160, 165, and 170 basis points above respective Treasury notes yields. Three of the eight investors, accounting for $65 million of the total placement, were large institutions with strong market reputations for credit diligence and expertise in the financial services sector.

In its next step, Comdisco needed to finalize its refinancing transaction. Armed with this successful private placement, the company then returned to the public market. Its credibility in the private market now gained the company timing advantages in raising capital. Soon it had successfully completed the financing at spreads just below those achieved in the privately placed transaction. In effect, Comdisco had employed the private market's more reasoned evaluation to reposition itself in an otherwise unfriendly public market. Thus it successfully completed its refinancing while meeting the objective of a lowered cost of funds.

In addition, to ensure the financing process goes smoothly, a company needs to be the hub of network organizations where it establishes relationships with other organizations that have the potential to add value. This is best known as a *strategic alliance*. Its partnering organizations may be funds seekers, universities, investors, or even competitors. Strategic alliances enable networked companies to exploit economies of scale to reduce required investment/risk. They also enable both parties to adopt positions beyond what either would take on individually. It is no wonder, then, that industries that are R&D intensive—like biotechnology, electronics, and semiconductors—and that have to keep up with rapidly changing technology need to make strategic alliances.

The value-creating drivers—brand, service, and process—should not only create value for investors and external customers, but also become a firm foundation of *internal* customers—the company's people. An organization's marketers must be its people. Functional arrogance within the company has to be avoided. Everyone must regard shareholder value as the best ultimate objective.

In summary, we conclude that these three value-creating principles—brand, service and process—are the real drivers enabling a company to win its fair share of investors' hearts.

## NOTES

1. See Justin Fox, "America's Most Admired Companies: What's So Great about GE?" *Fortune*, February 2002.
2. Source: www.kotlermarketing.com/resources/miltonkotler /pearls/p38.html.
3. See a complete explanation about brand equity by David A. Aaker, *Managing Brand Equity: Capitalizing on the Value of a Brand Name*, New York: Free Press, 1991.
4. Source: www.ogilvypr.com.
5. The discussion about public relations can be seen in Chapter 7 in the marketing mix section.
6. See the elaboration of brand identity concept in David A. Aaker, *Building Strong Brands*, New York: Free Press, 1996.

7. Peter Lynch with John Rothchild, *One Up on Wall Street: How to Use What You Already Know to Make Money in the Market*, New York: Fireside, 2000, p. 207.

8. Ibid.

9. Source: Dennis Emerick and William White, "The Case for Private Placements: How Sophisticated Investors Add Value to Corporate Debt Issuers," in Donald H. Chew Jr., ed., *The New Corporate Finance: Where Theory Meets Practice*, Boston: McGraw-Hill/Irwin, 1999, p. 353.

10. The Disney case was extracted from Philip J. Adkins, "Brand Monetisation," in Raymond Perrier, ed., *Brand Valuation*, London: Premier Books, 1997, pp. 137–140.

11. Valerie A. Zeithaml, A. Parasuraman, and Leonard A. Berry, *Delivering Quality Service: Balancing Customer Perceptions and Expectations*, New York: Free Press, 1990.

12. Robert G. Eccles, Robert H. Herz, E. Mary Keegan, and David M. H. Phillips, *The Value Reporting Revolution: Moving beyond the Earnings Game*, New York: John Wiley & Sons, 2001, pp. 161–183.

13. Emerick and White, *Case for Private Placements*, pp. 346–354.

14. www.coca-cola.com.

15. Source: Daniel Kadlec, "WorldCom," *Time*, July 8, 2002.

16. This case has been extracted from Eccles et al. *Value Reporting Revolution*, pp. 161–183.

17. Emerick and White, *Case for Private Placements*.

# PART FOUR

# EPILOGUE

# 9

# Get Your Marketing Right!

Attracting capital is never easy. A company has to compete for capital not only in its own industry but against everyone else competing for capital whose opportunities and risk profiles are similar. To make matters worse, the capital market is burdened with speculators who have no real interest in long-term company fundamentals. Their interest lies in gaining profits from short-term price movements.

Marketing theory and practice can help companies vie for capital more effectively. The capital seeker must research the most appropriate sources of funding and not waste time calling on every possible funder. The company must adapt its business case and presentation to each funder based on its understanding of what each funder values and is seeking. The company must present convincing evidence of its ability to deliver on its promises.

Companies at an early stage of growth usually raise funds from family and friends, by bootstrapping, or from angel investors. Such ventures represent the highest level of business risk. The capital seeker must normally undertake debt finance, namely promising a specific return to the investors. Yet debt finance must be kept down and equity funding sought to the extent possible.

The small percentage of entrepreneurial firms that do survive the start-up phase and climb into higher growth will need to raise private equity to realize the enterprise's potential value. External private equity funding will most likely have to come from venture capital firms. But VC funding can prove difficult to attract, as the company is probably still risky, even though it may have a promising future. A perception of high risk will limit the pool of potential investors to a small number. High-risk new businesses are rendered off-limits to the largest pools of available capital within mutual funds, insurance company portfolios, and pension funds that are all constrained in their investing by governments or their own bylaws.

Companies can gain access to institutional investor funding—mainly from banks, mutual funds, pension funds, and insurance companies—once they have had a successful IPO. These investors generally like established businesses that offer them liquidity in the marketplace and readily evaluated risks and rewards.

Sound marketing is essential for any company seeking to take full advantage of its funding sources. With the right strategy, supported by appropriate tactics, funds seekers can increase the probability of obtaining the desired funds from the capital market.

In the first stage, a company's task is to develop a capital market *strategy*. Strategy involves three successive steps: segmentation, targeting, and positioning. Effective *segmentation* requires creatively clustering the prospective investors according to their diverse needs, perceptions, preferences, and behaviours. *Targeting* involves the decision of which segments to pursue. Finally, the company must *position* itself in potential investors' minds to gain their interest and commitment. Investors need to have a clear picture in their minds of the capital-seeking company's "being" so that it appears attractive and credible.

In the second stage, the company develops *tactics* for engaging in the capital market. It utilizes differentiation, marketing mix, and selling. *Differentiation* is the core tactic as it holds the key to standing out from competitors. This is done through a a unique blending of content, context, and infrastructure aimed at producing a strong mind share and heart share among target investors. The company then creates a *marketing mix* that meaningfully combines the company's offer and access. To implement the tactics, *selling* is now required. Selling is intended to convince investors of the benefits stemming from a mutually beneficial long-term relationship.

Finally, the funds seeker must ensure that it obtains its desired *value* in the capital market. The three elements required for this are brand, service, and process. To avoid the commodity trap, a company must develop a strong *brand*, its value indicator. Next, it must meet or even exceed investor's expectations by delivering good *service*. The last element, *process*, allows a company to deliver value to its investors through various activity chains involving delivering information and performance metrics to its investors.

In practice, strategy, tactics and value must all be balanced. They will then work together to win the investors' mind, market, and heart shares.

# INDEX